THE NEW DEAL AND THE SOUTH

The New Deal and the South

Essays by
FRANK FREIDEL
PETE DANIEL
J. WAYNE FLYNT
ALAN BRINKLEY
HARVARD SITKOFF
NUMAN V. BARTLEY

Edited by
JAMES C. COBB
and
MICHAEL V. NAMORATO

UNIVERSITY PRESS OF MISSISSIPPI
Jackson

THIS VOLUME HAS BEEN SPONSORED BY
THE UNIVERSITY OF MISSISSIPPI

Library of Congress Cataloging in Publication Data
Main entry under title:

The New Deal and the South.

   Papers presented at the Ninth Annual Chancellor's
Symposium on Southern History held Oct. 12–14, 1983, at
the University of Mississippi and sponsored by the
University of Mississippi.
   Bibliography: p.
   Includes index.
   1. Southern States—History—1865–1951—Congresses.
2. New Deal, 1933–1939—Congresses.   I. Freidel, Frank
Burt.   II. Cobb, James C. (James Charles), 1947–
III. Namorato, Michael V.   IV. Chancellor's Symposium on
Southern History (9th : 1983 : University of Mississippi)
V. University of Mississippi.
F215.N49   1984   975'.042   84-5109
ISBN 0-87805-218-6
ISBN 0-87805-219-4 (pbk.)

Dedicated to

PORTER L. FORTUNE, JR.

Chancellor

The University of Mississippi

Contents

Preface

It was entirely appropriate that the ninth annual Chancellor's Symposium on Southern History dealt with the topic "The New Deal and the South." Fifty years ago, Franklin D. Roosevelt launched his New Deal to combat the worst economic depression in American history. The New Deal affected every area of American life and society and had a particularly significant impact on the South. In an era when the merits of big government are often hotly debated, the legacy of the New Deal remains visible nationally and within the South. On October 12–14, 1983, scholars from across the United States converged on the University of Mississippi campus and, for three days, analyzed the New Deal and its effects on the South. The papers that follow were presented at that conference.

Organizing and implementing a conference of this size requires the support of many people. We would like especially to thank the Division of Research Programs at the National Endowment for the Humanities and Dr. Cora Norman and her staff at the Mississippi Committee for the Humanities for their generous financial support. Their cooperation, assistance, and encouragement went far beyond anything we could expect.

Our gratitude is also extended to the moderators/commentators of the conference who were asked to introduce the speakers, comment on their papers, and moderate audience discussion. Paul Conkin, Roy Scott, Tom Terrill, Neil McMillen,

John Kirby, and Jack Temple Kirby performed their assigned tasks in a highly professional manner.

For the last eighteen months, our colleagues in the Department of History and the Center for the Study of Southern Culture listened to us, worked with us, and assisted us in carrying out the many details associated with the symposium. To each of them, we extend our warmest thanks, knowing full well that they will expect us to return their favors at the appropriate time.

Finally, on behalf of the Department of History and the Center for the Study of Southern Culture, we express our deepest thanks to the man who supported the Symposium from its very beginnings in 1975. Throughout the last nine years, he has consistently supported and sustained our efforts. As a token of our appreciation and respect, we have dedicated this volume to him. Moreover, the Department of History has resolved unanimously that from this time on, the name of the annual conference will be—"The Chancellor Porter L. Fortune, Jr., Symposium on Southern History."

JAMES C. COBB
MICHAEL V. NAMORATO

THE NEW DEAL AND THE SOUTH

Introduction

JAMES C. COBB AND MICHAEL V. NAMORATO

Much of the study of southern history since the Civil War has centered on the question of continuity and change. For many years, the continuity/change debate focused on whether the Civil War displaced a planter elite that has been the dominant force in southern politics for two generations. In his 1941 synthesis, *The Mind of the South*, Wilbur J. Cash argued that the planter and his ethos had survived the conflict intact.[1] Cash even saw the influence of the planter in the late nineteenth-century crusade for an industrialized "New South," arguing that "Progress stood quite accurately for a sort of new charge at Gettysburg." Behind the building and Babbitry of "The Atlanta Spirit," the twentieth-century descendant of the New South ethos, Cash was certain he could hear "the gallop of Jeb Stuart's cavalrymen."

A decade later, C. Vann Woodward reached a different set of conclusions in *Origins of the New South, 1877–1913*.[2] Woodward contended that from the ashes of the Civil War rose a new breed of leader representing an ascendant commercial middle class with a philosophy and goals clearly distinguishable from those of the displaced planters.

Although Woodward's interpretation held sway for a number of years, recent examinations of the political economy of the late nineteenth century have affirmed many of Cash's observations. In their respective studies of late nineteenth-century North Carolina and Alabama, Dwight B. Billings, Jr., and Jonathan M.

3

Wiener argued that a coalition of planters and industrialists took steps to insure that the New South could be constructed on a plantation foundation. Some advocates of industrialization had spoken initially of a balanced economy wherein independently owned, diversified farms would feed predominantly industrial urban centers. In the face of planter reluctance to yield power and the threat of political and social upheaval posed by the agrarian movements of the 1880s and 1890s, however, New South spokesmen recognized the special interests of affluent landholders and gave their assurances that industrial development would not undermine the sharecropping system by siphoning away farm labor. Nor would it engender class consciousness, and thereby threaten the stability essential not only to planter hegemony but to the future attraction of external investment capital.

In *The Social Origins of the New South*, Wiener contended that a conservative coalition of planter and manufacturing interests has led Alabama down the "Prussian Road" to industrial expansion.[3] In *Planters and the Making of a New South*, Billings found a similar pattern of "conservative modernization" in North Carolina whose economic development he compared to that of Germany and Japan in the nineteenth century.[4] In both states, the social and political structure remained agrarian oriented and economic growth depended on low-wage, labor-intensive industries, most of which were involved in processing raw materials or agricultural products. The findings of Wiener and Billings suggested that as the twentieth century began, the South remained a closed society heavily influenced if not dominated by conservative planters.

The plantation stood at the center of southern society, shaping not only its economy, but its social and political structure as well. The region's middle class fed on commerce with the countryside, buying the planter's crops for export beyond the region and handling the importation of the manufactured goods and supplies that he purchased. The cash-poor agricultural economy showed little prospect for modernization and the rural location and small scale of manufacturing created little pressure for either mechanization (by reducing the farm labor force) or diversification (by creating fast-growing urban markets for foodstuffs). Meanwhile, racial antagonism and disfranchisement neutralized lower class whites and blacks, creating a social and political hierarchy dominated by planters, merchants, and small manufacturers.[5]

As the South entered the New Deal era, its economic and political structure was dominated by a figure described by Ralph McGill as "a certain type, small-town rich man" who "lived in the best house, on the best hill in town" and owned, "according to his geographic location," either the gin or the cotton warehouse, the turpentine works, or the tobacco warehouse.[6] Wherever he lived, he was often a director of the local bank. The small-town rich man sold food, seed, and farm supplies. He controlled credit and not only dominated local politics but enjoyed entreé to the governor, his senators, and his congressman. The man McGill described was the pivotal figure in an economy where both small town and, to a significant extent, urban commerce remained dependent on the fortunes of agriculture, a reality reflected by the dispersion of political power across the rural and small-town countryside. Within such a political context, the dominant priorities were white supremacy with the small-town rich man at the top of the heap, minimal taxation, laissez-faire government, and labor stability. McGill asserted that these sinister local barons and their values were "in trouble" as the New Deal era began.

Recent historical research indicates that the New Deal era was a crucial period in southern history, a time when the foundations of social and political stagnation began to crumble. Coupled wih the reinforcing influences of World War II, the New Deal seems to have been the most powerful force for change in the South since the Civil War. In *The Emergence of the New South, 1913–1945,* George B. Tindall concluded that the New Deal shook "the social and economic power structure" of the south.[7]

Similarly, in his *The South: A History*, I. A. Newby observed that "The New Deal was a national endeavor, but it included the most systematic effort ever made to tackle the special economic problems of the South."[8] It was during the New Deal years that Dixie won unwelcome recognition as the "Nation's Number One Economic Problem." The Agricultural Adjustment Act, the Farm Security Act, and the Tennessee Valley Authority, to name but a few, were destined to have a major impact on the South's economy. In *FDR and the South*, Frank Freidel concluded that while Roosevelt "never sufficiently challenged southern traditions of white supremacy to create problems for himself, he did back economic changes to improve the lot of the underprivileged, white and black alike."[9]

Most historians agree that, while it triggered no revolution, the New Deal became an important influence for change in a region where the socio-economic and political hierarchy was committed to the status quo. This volume provides the first comprehensive assessment of the New Deal's impact on the South. The contributors offer a fuller explanation of both the limitations of the New Deal's short-term effect and of its role in inducing or accelerating the long-term economic, racial, and political changes that produced dramatic alterations in "the southern way of life."

In the first essay, Freidel describes the New Deal era as "one of the most important phases in the modernization of the South." He cites the New Deal's role in accelerating the "mechanization and overall modernization of southern agriculture, its alleviation of some of the worst of the region's poverty, and its contributions in education, housing, and employment." Although he concedes that blacks received less than their fair share of New Deal assistance, Freidel emphasizes that they did receive at least a portion of the tangible benefits of the Roosevelt program as well as a much more generous supply of hope. The expectations raised by the New Deal, coupled with the migration of southern blacks to the North where they could vote, gradually increased the mounting pressures which began the transformation of the Democratic Party's stance on racial equality. Freidel does not see the New Deal as revolutionary, but he describes it as a time when many of the seeds of change sown in an earlier era grew to maturity under the influence of an expanded federal presence and support structure. The New Deal served as an important link between the first New South created in the post-Reconstruction decades and the much newer Sunbelt South that emerged in the 1970s.

The first step in the creation of the Sunbelt South was the modernization of southern agriculture. The boll weevil, which invaded Texas in the early 1890s, had conquered the entire Deep South by 1923, leaving in its wake crop devastation so severe that failing farms began to disgorge large numbers of tenants and sharecroppers. The onset of the depression accelerated this trend, but, as Pete Daniel observed in a recent article, the major influence in the "transformation" of the rural South was the Agricultural Adjustment Administration's acreage reduction program.[10] In the first seven years of AAA operations, the thirteen cotton states lost over 30 percent of their sharecroppers and 12 percent of other tenants. AAA crop reduction subsidies not only made sharecroppers superfluous but provided cash for farm consolidation. As tractors replaced tenants, the shrinking farm economy focused attention on the need for industrialization as a means to provide jobs for the farm labor surplus and a market for the goods and services provided by the suddenly threatened commercial and professional middle class.

In his essay, Daniel stresses the impact of the New Deal in altering for thousands of southerners not only the way they made a living but the way they lived. The crop reduction policies of the Agricultural Adjustment Administration triggered the forces of mechanization, consolidation, and corporatization within southern agriculture. The result was a vast "enclosure movement" wherein "many southerners, black and white, hesitantly left the countryside, paused in towns and cities nearby, and moved on out of the South never to return." The traditional relationship with the landlord gave way to the twenty-seven federal agencies that "took up the slack as paternalistic provider." In the long run, many of the uprooted sharecroppers would find refuge in the army, defense industries, or other plants lured to the region by an aggressive, greatly expanded industrial development effort. In the short run, however, the primary beneficiaries of AAA policies were the large landholders and corporations rather than the beleaguered small farmers struggling to avoid tenancy or an even more desperate group, the tenants themselves.

The Roosevelt Era brought more immediate gains to southern industrial workers. F. Ray Marshall cited the favorable impact of New Deal legislation on southern unions and the overall status and working conditions of southern workers.[11] Tindall observed that while there had been no "revolutionary transformation," the New Deal Era focused greater attention on the plight of southern labor and "left a legacy of permanent unionism and minimum standards set by legislation."

In his essay on the New Deal and southern labor, Wayne Flynt concludes that the Roosevelt program did make a difference to southern workers. The federal government's support for collective bargaining accelerated union growth and discouraged the antiunion practices for which southern states and communities were infamous. Flynt also finds that the New Deal reduced regional wage differentials, speeded changes in race relations, and encouraged greater political participation by southern labor and greater liberalism on the part of southern politicians. Still, Flynt concludes that these changes amounted to little more than a beginning and that in the wake of the New Deal southern labor remained vulnerable to intimidation and racial and economic exploitation.

As the New Deal began, no group in the nation was more vulnerable to intimidation and exploitation than southern blacks. Raymond Wolters, Jr., concluded in *Negroes and the Great Depression* "that black people received less than a fair share of economic aid from some important New Deal recovery agencies" and thus "suffered the inevitable fate of a disorganized minority when they failed to participate fully in the recovery stimulated by World War II and maintained by massive postwar military spending."[12] In *A New Deal for Blacks,* Harvard Sitkoff conceded the limited nature of black progress under the New Deal, but, nonetheless saw the 1930s as a time when black expectations had been raised and the seeds of future progress had been planted.[13]

Sitkoff reiterates this theme in his essay, emphasizing the limitations imposed by a heritage of racism, black poverty, and powerlessness, as well as the New Deal's dependence on local program administrators and Roosevelt's determination to put economic recovery ahead of racial and other reforms. Relief was insufficient and inequitably distributed, but such federal assistance as they did receive helped southern blacks to survive the depression. Although "the greatest mass of black southerners remained in 1941, as they had been in 1933, victims of a brutally inequitable caste system," they nonetheless embraced Franklin Roosevelt and the New Deal. According to Sitkoff, by making a number of highly visible appointments of both white liberals and blacks, expressing concern and respect for blacks, and encouraging his wife Eleanor's active interest in racial reform, Roosevelt helped to create a spirit of hope that "transformed the despair, and discouragement, and dreadful apathy of black southerners into a fighting conviction of a better world that would soon and surely be achieved."

Not all southern whites shared the enthusiasm for Roosevelt shown by southern blacks. Although New Deal largesse encouraged many southern political leaders to swear fealty to President Franklin D. Roosevelt, the growing liberalization of the Democratic Party and the expanded federal bureaucracy with its expanded regulatory responsibility helped to escalate tensions between Dixie and Washington. In *The Rise of Massive Resistance,* Numan V. Bartley concluded that anti-New Deal sentiment, emanating from the "doctor-lawyer-merchant governing class" provided a seedbed of conservative protest linked to the

1948 Dixiecrat revolt, the Citizens Council/Massive Resistance movement of the 1950s, and, to some extent, the growth of a Republican base in the South.[14]

In his essay, Alan Brinkley pursues this theme by analyzing the New Deal's failure to give the South a rational, class-based politics. Brinkley notes that Franklin Roosevelt was far more concerned with maintaining his ties to powerful southern politicos from Congress all the way down to the courthouse than with starting a political revolution in the South. Gratitude for federal aid and vocal support for the New Deal were far too commonplace among otherwise conservative southern leaders to serve as a litmus test of emerging liberalism. With its simmering racial anxieties and its growing fear of external assaults on the southern way of life, the South provided a peculiarly unfertile environment for political progressivism. Dixie did have its political mavericks in the 1930s but the force of this fervent, but diffuse, insurgency was as often directed at Washington as at the traditional power structure at the state level. Brinkley believes that this insurgency derived more from Populist than from Progressive traditions and "looked with equal hostility at the conservative aristocrats who dominated southern politics and the social democratic liberals who were building a powerful and intrusive new federal bureaucracy." Southern political insurgency represented a much more formidable force than did southern liberalism, but it was a force which Franklin Roosevelt often found difficult to contain, much less exploit.

In assessing the overall impact of the New Deal on southern politics Brinkley concurs with the other contributors in stressing long- rather than short-term effects. He cites internal factors like the transformation of plantation agriculture, a change that shifted political power away from the Black Belt and ultimately toward the cities, where many black sharecroppers had fled and where the early ferment for civil rights activism first became noticeable. More important still, however, was the New Deal's influence outside the South. Abandonment of the two-thirds requirement for nomination stripped the South of its traditional veto power while the attraction of an overwhelming majority of northern black voters and an intensified courtship of organized labor further "northernized" the Democratic party. Like southern conservatives of the 1930s, Brinkley links these phenomena to the civil rights movement, the long-dreaded external assault that struck at the racial and political traditions on which the southern way of life rested and without which it could exist only in much altered form.

The New Deal's significance as a "turning point" in southern history must be assessed broadly in terms of its racial, economic, and political impact. As Daniel shows, the New Deal became a crucial influence in transforming the rural South, especially in terms of mechanization of agriculture and the collapse of the sharecropping system. These developments, in turn, led to an accelerated effort to sell the South to industrial investors. Sitkoff describes the New Deal period as one when a Democratic party now accountable to black voters and an increasingly hopeful and restive black population began to exert pressure for racial change. Brinkley depicts the New Deal as a source of political tension because it forced southern Democrats to weigh their party loyalties and the resulting federal aid benefits against their economic conservatism and their concern that the New Deal might represent the first phase of a movement to subject the South to a "Second Reconstruction." In a recent article, William N. Parker emphasized the importance of the New Deal as well as World War II and other physical, technological, and extraneous market and political events in breaking the back of "southern institutional peculiarity" and allowing the region's "energies and resources . . . to be merged with the national society."[15]

In the concluding essay, Numan V. Bartley argues persuasively that historians who have focused so intently on the immediate post-Civil War decades might better shift their attention to a new "crucial decade" approximating the years 1935–1945.

Citing many of the changes identified by the other contributors, Bartley gives particular attention to the collapse of the South's paternalistic labor system and to changes in the behavior of working people and their attitudes toward work. Bartley observes that "commodity labor replaced the more personal labor relations of an earlier era and a growth-oriented metropolitan elite replaced a county-seat elite committed to traditional social stability." The ascendance of metropolitan leaders intent on integrating their local and state economies into the national economy led them to champion growth as "the panacea for southern public problems." The expanded crusade for industrial development used the desire of an underemployed agricultural labor surplus for steady work to entice northern capital to the South. The resultant shift to industrialization and the racial and political changes set in motion by the New Deal modified the region's "social structure, ideology, and personal interrelationships." Intensified by World War II, these changes were profound, but as Bartley and most scholars agree, they remain "ill understood."

When the essays in this volume are considered collectively, several common characteristics appear. One is the frequent use of phrases like "sowed the seeds" which suggests a limited short-term influence but a larger cumulative, long-term one. The most significant and relatively immediate effect was the transformation of southern agriculture, a phenomenon that swept thousands from the land and deposited them at least temporarily in the region's towns and cities, which were for many but a way station on a trek that would lead ultimately to the urban North. The mechanization and consolidation of agriculture altered the South's economic priorities dramatically, simultaneously facilitating and almost necessitating a much more intensive emphasis on industrialization. The region's relatively anemic commercial and professional classes, once linked inextricably to the plantation system of agriculture, now looked elsewhere for their livelihood, specifically toward a broader industrial base that would expand the region's consuming class and strengthen its consuming potential. Ralph McGill's small-town rich man hardly vanished under a deluge of new factories, and, in fact, much of the South's newly won industry was quite compatible with his economic and political philosophy. Still, once the old plantation system and the labor system on which it rested began to disappear, the influence of the rural, small-town planter/agribusinessman was certain to wane. In the wake of World War II, the reins of power passed to a dynamic, metropolitan elite who saw their own and their region's future largely in terms of a more diversified, integrated economy operating in much closer proximity to the nation's economic mainstream. Ultimately, such a vision encouraged a more moderate position on race as well as other reforms designed to streamline government and create the potential for a life-style acceptable to an expanding middle class.

Because culmination of so many of the trends set in motion by the New Deal awaited the end of World War II, an important question emerges from these essays. The war greatly expanded federal spending, stimulated industrialization, and boosted per capita income in the South. How closely would the New Deal be linked to significant changes in the South's economic, social, and political structure were it not for wartime changes that not only moved the South in the directions suggested by the New Deal but quickened the pace of its journey? How rapidly would mechanization of agriculture have proceeded had the armed services, defense jobs, and outmigration in search of these jobs not increased competition for southern labor? To what extent did the war alone contribute to a deeper concern about civil rights among northern democratic leaders? Actually, the New Deal might also be viewed as one of a series of major events and trends stretching from the boll weevil invasion of the 1920s through the upheaval of war in the 1940s. At any rate, World War II seems to rank as the premier event of this "turning period" of southern history and both the war's impact on the South and the relationship of that impact to the New Deal deserve the close scholarly attention they are beginning to receive.

These essays also point to the New Deal's influence outside the South. The changes which the New Deal wrought in American society at large brought mounting external pressure for changes in the South. The affirmation of collective bargaining cleared the way for new union forays into Dixie. Ironically, the strengthening of organized labor in the North may have facilitated the efforts of southern industrial development leaders to entice labor-intensive, low-wage industries to the South. Organized labor also played a major role in a reshaped Democratic party. If the New Deal failed to create a "rational," class- and interest-group-based politics in the South, it came much closer to doing so outside the region. The result was a Democratic party oriented more to the working classes and the poor and a party whose growing concern for blacks led ultimately to major federal efforts in behalf of southern blacks. These new policies led to significant gains for blacks and, in the process, to enough disaffection among traditionally Democratic whites to create a genuinely competitive political atmosphere in a region that had once been a Democratic monolith. Finally, the New Deal ushered in nearly a half-century of relatively uninterrupted bipartisan reliance on federal intervention as a response to social injustice, economic deprivation, and human blight. Despite its limitations, the New Deal helped to make the United States into a nation where the South's most appalling excesses and severest problems would no longer seem tolerable or insolvable.

In one way or another, all of the essays in this volume link the changes induced by the New Deal—mechanization of agriculture, mobilization of black voters, support for collective bargaining and expansion of federal influence—to the modernization that ultimately bore fruit in the contemporary Sunbelt South. Yet, the contributors also emphasize the limitations of the changes induced by the New Deal. These limitations also provide an important means of understanding the contemporary South. Uneven growth, lingering poverty and discrimination, educational deficiencies, and persistent regional wage differ-

There were limitations, too!

entials are but a few of the problems of the New Deal era that still exist in the age of the Sunbelt. On the other hand, however, the restricted nature of the changes induced by the New Deal has contributed to the Sunbelt's strengths as well as its shortcomings. The parts of the South that grew most rapidly in the wake of World War II owed much of that growth to the enduring conservatism, continuity, and stability that characterized the region. Industrialists chose southern locations primarily because of the region's abundance of cheap, nonunion labor, its regressive, pro-business tax structure, and its reputation for conservative government. Many of the key elements of the favorable business climate lauded by investors around the nation and the world remained in place in the 1970s and 1980s because both the New Deal and the subsequent war experience failed to trigger an immediate and thorough-going transformation of southern society. While agricultural modernization, improvements in income, and other changes induced by the New Deal and accelerated by World War II may have been prerequisites for the emergence of the Sunbelt, the conditions left in place by these two events are also crucial to any meaningful understanding of the South in the 1980s.

The essays presented here provide a much-needed assessment of the New Deal's impact on the South. Both the scholar and the general reader should find in this book information and analysis necessary to better understand the New Deal's legacy to the contemporary South, a legacy of change superimposed on a fading but still visible heritage of change deferred.

The South and the New Deal

FRANK FREIDEL

The era of the New Deal was one of the most important phases in the modernization of the South. Viewing the United States as a whole, a distinguished University of Virginia economist, Herbert Stein, has suggested that even if the New Deal had never taken place the economy today nonetheless would probably function in as modern a fashion as those of other western nations. Undoubtedly Stein is correct, yet the question remains when would the changes have taken place that distinguish the economy and society of today from that of the New Era of President Calvin Coolidge? Applied to the South, both Stein's question and the answer might be the same. The roots of much of the spectacular change in the South can be found in the New Deal, as the area has been transformed from being regarded as the nation's number one economic problem into what is looked upon with envy from New England to the Pacific Northwest as the burgeoning Sunbelt. This is not to overrate the importance of the New Deal. Certainly the changes in the South since have been far more spectacular than those between Redemption and the inauguration of Franklin D. Roosevelt.[1]

The earlier changes did much to prepare the South for the New Deal, principally, as is commonplace through the drive for industrialization and progressive reform. Also, they carried with them rigidities that added to the urgent need for the changes that came in the 1930s. Up into the New Deal, one finds serious

17

limitations growing out of the assumptions and institutions that
southern leaders in the last decades of the nineteenth-century
and at the beginning of the twentieth century hailed as achieve-
ments.

First, there were the economic bases. Southern leaders had
tried to bring prosperity through industrialization—the famous
New South Creed of Henry Grady and the *Atlanta Constitution*.
They sought to lure factories from the North through offering
lower operating costs, and in so doing forced the southern workers to subsist at a level well below that of their northern counterparts. In agriculture they sought to compete too, trying to produce cotton for the world market in competition with the cheap
labor of Brazil, Egypt, India, and elsewhere. The returns for
those who chopped cotton or picked it on a sharecropping or crop
lien system, were a bare subsistence, and for most landowners no
luxurious way of life. Southern political leaders sought redress
through seeking more industry, and, echoing the refrains of Calhoun, they called for lower tariffs or free trade to liberate the
cotton producers bound by world prices from the tyranny of
having to purchase protected northern manufactured goods.
There were other complaints, of course, dating from the era of
Tom Watson and the Southern Populists—the additional tyranny
of being dependent upon northern capital, and having to submit
to higher freight rates on southern railroads and base-point pric-
ing of some commodities. Birmingham steel, so much cheaper to
produce, had to sell at the price of Pittsburgh steel plus transportation charges. What altogether these familiar facts mean is that
the chief economic asset of the South was the fact that southern
people worked for less than those in the rest of the United States.
These conditions, increasingly resented, extended up into the
New Deal. When George B. Tindall took over from the sociologist Rupert B. Vance the task of writing *The Emergence of the
New South*, he kept several of Vance's chapter titles, and I sus-
pect among them was one on the New Deal years, "Dilemmas of
a Colonial Economy." These static conditions, growing out of

attempts to stimulate the southern economy, were barely tolerable in the 1920s; when the Great Depression came, they were even more painful.

Second, the static conditions required a relatively static society. To help sustain that rejection of change was the myth of an earlier, more genteel way of life, of a classic democracy (or rather oligarchy) in which each assumed one's proper station in life—of a southern Atlantis sunk beneath the waves with the collapse of the Confederacy. In the 1930s, the myth assumed its most alluring form, first as a book and then as a motion picture, even today converting probably more Yankee viewers than southerners, Margaret Mitchell's *Gone With the Wind*. Preserved and still relatively intact in the 1930s was the heritage of "differentness," the premise based four-square upon the dogma of *Plessy* v. *Ferguson*, that separate was equal, and upon the Atlanta Compromise of Booker T. Washington, that black hands (at least temporarily) would restrict themselves to the labors of Noah's son Ham and his descendants. To the myth of the Lost Cause was added that of Redemption which in turn blended into that of the New South. A generation of politicians whose greatest claim upon the electorate was their leadership of the grey battalions gave way to those who kept warm memories of the glories of the Confederacy and shuddered at the shame of Reconstruction—all in defense of the status quo.

The popular politics of the South continued thus down into the 1930s. Progressivism in the South as well as the North meant in part clean government, and the southerners interpreted that to mean keeping the allegedly corrupting influence of blacks out of politics, and putting the force of law behind segregation. There was something of biblical mysticism that crept into the rhetoric, as though the existing order were divinely ordained.

Along with the rhetoric on white supremacy often went appeals to protect southern womanhood—white womanhood that is—although already in the 1920s with suffrage guaranteed them, some of the southern white women Democrats were firmly as-

serting that they did not want to be relegated to a pedestal but
insisted upon being active in politics. A few were.

Minnie Fisher Cunningham, who in the summer of 1928 had
the temerity to run in the Texas primary for United States
Senator, attended the meeting of the Regular Democrats in Aus-
tin, and was pained by what she heard. There were lots of nice
regulars there who liked her, but also those who had fought
suffrage and were "out again":

> They made speeches—old fashioned oratorical speeches—
> all about the Confederacy and the "gallant soldiers who wore
> the gray" and "the wicked and iniquitous carpet baggers" who
> oppressed them—and the "dirty black niggers" who were
> elevated to rule over the "noble womanhood"—no I mean
> "*pure* and noble womanhood of the South" by these same
> naughty carpet baggers—Honestly Dorothy I haven't heard
> such rot since the world war & I had begun to hope I never
> *would* hear it again. . . .
> And then I talked to them for about ten minutes telling them
> a few things I thought it might benefit them to hear—such as
> this election came in 1928 not 1861—and that I'd confide to
> them the priceless lesson I had learned on the stump this
> summer to wit—it takes *votes* to win elections.[2]

Thereupon, that afternoon the Texas Regular Democrats
elected Mrs. Cunningham vice chairman of the state campaign.
Several score women like her, active in Democratic politics,
were to receive significant administrative positions in the New
Deal.

By the 1930s the United Confederate Veterans were dwindling
rapidly. The xenophobia of the Lost Cause was waning, but the
road to reunion was far longer and bumpier than one would
surmise from Paul Buck's Pulitzer Prize monograph which appeared in 1937. Franklin D. Roosevelt, speaking at Gettysburg
three years earlier, had blamed the "Brother's War" in part on
lack of communication, inveighed against "the selfishness of sectionalism," and with some truth asserted, "It has been left to us of
this generation to see the healing made permanent." Time was

perhaps the most important factor, symbolized by the fact that in 1913, the blue and gray, averaging less than 70 years, engaged in cussing and fisticuffs rather than agree to a joint reunion; in 1938, averaging 94 years of age, 530 of the ex-Confederates and 1,420 of the Grand Army of the Republic, met to celebrate the seventy-fifth anniversary of the Battle of Gettysburg. They paraded in a line of wheelchairs, pushed by Boy Scouts. It was only at that point that brotherhood came to prevail among the blue and the gray.[3]

Along with the sectional healing, other seeds of change, to borrow the apt title of Wilma Dykeman's and James Stokeley's biography of Will Alexander, were being planted in the pre-New Deal years. Some were factors from outside the South which were to have long-range effects. A prime example was the cutting off of immigration and the increased industrial activity beginning with the First World War, which brought southern blacks for the first time in considerable numbers into northern factories. The blacks created sizeable bridgeheads in cities like Chicago and Detroit to which additional friends and relatives moved from the South through the prosperous twenties. World War I also brought the construction of the Wilson Dam at Muscle Shoals on the Tennessee River, with its promise of cheap power and fertilizer. As the waters, little used, ran over the spillways in the 1920s, it provided a convincing object lesson for many southerners of the need for the intervention, if not of Henry Ford and private initiative, of the Federal government to stimulate the southern economy. The long-running debate in Congress over Muscle Shoals through the 1920s helped modify the thinking of many devotees of states' rights dogma.

Above all, the changes were coming among the younger generation of southerners. The large Democratic minority in Congress was for the most part from the South, and looked back with nostalgia to the brief years when it had been the majority and had enacted President Wilson's New Freedom program. The New Freedom, while it ideologically enveloped states' rights and white supremacy, had also brought the Federal Reserve system with easier credit and an array of federal grants-in-aid programs. This legislation, while subtly undermining states' rights through setting standards of quality, won support through bringing federal funds (much of the money from the northeast) to promote highway building, agricultural education, and farm bureau county agents. It is not surprising that practically all the southern politicians regarded themselves as Wilsonians, committed to the preservation if not expansion of the New Freedom programs that would bring more money into the South.

In the southern universities through the Progressive Era and the New Era several generations of students were exposed to the progressive view of history, political science, economics, society, and the law. At the University of North Carolina, the historian J. G. de Roulhac Hamilton, bringing to perfection the W. A. Dunning view of southern history, staunchly defended the old order, while in contrast the sociologist of the South, Howard Odum, through systematically organizing the facts in the most approved progressive fashion, and asking, but not answering, embarrassing questions, cautiously prepared the way for change. Odum and his counterparts throughout the South were developing far more of a following than the perpetuators of the Dunning school. There were those too, beginning as clergymen of a "social gospel" bent, who like Aubrey Williams and Will Alexander gradually became iconoclasts, not only questioning southern dogma, but proposing bold new departures. Almost unnoticed were the younger black leaders, many of them in the North and others at Howard, Fisk, Atlanta and other black institutions in the South. They had long since abandoned Booker T. Washington and were quietly chipping away at the walls of segregation. There was also the contribution of that exciting group of young southern men of letters, the Agrarians, who in *I'll Take My Stand* (1930) rejected the industrialism encroaching from the North and extolled the regional values of the South.[4]

By the end of the New Era, the seeds of southern change that

these varying views represented were sprouting. The New Deal
was to provide a hothouse in which some of them could burgeon.
The chief gardener in that hothouse was no southerner, but a
New Yorker, Franklin D. Roosevelt.

Roosevelt and the southern Democratic leaders were very important to each other. There was, of course, much opportunism
in the relationship, but that is the nature of politics. Without the
South, Roosevelt could not have obtained the presidential nomination in 1932. Conversely, the southern leaders had initially
turned to Roosevelt as the one realistic way to wrest control of
the party from the northern city bosses, the Catholic wets. At the
1932 convention they would have far preferred John Nance Garner or someone from the Deep South, but had they consented to
the blocking of Roosevelt they would have wound up with someone like Newton D. Baker, not very palatable to them. Garner
said it all when, releasing his delegates, he remarked to Sam
Rayburn, "Hell, I'll do anything to see the Democrats win one
more national election."[5]

Still, much more than opportunism was involved. Roosevelt,
during his seven years as assistant secretary of the navy in the
Wilson administration, served under that ardent southern progressive, Josephus Daniels, and came to know most of the southern Democrats, both young and old. By 1920, when he ran for
vice-president, he had absorbed almost all of their ideology.
During the years after his polio attack when, at Warm Springs,
Georgia, he was trying to regain use of his legs he kept his
political skills in top form. Certainly more than any other northern Democratic leader, he understood and empathized with the
southerners and their problems.

The views of the southern Wilsonians had become his—
progressive reform with a states' rights emphasis, encompassing
both industrialization and an ardent agrarianism. To a later generation, this mixture of views seems a mishmash of inconsistency,
but it pretty well sums up the state of mind in the early 1930s of
many southern liberals—not only of FDR's former chief, the

Bryan follower and Wilsonian, Josephus Daniels, but also of his son, Jonathan Daniels. It was the younger Daniels who brought literary grace to the views of the Southern sociologists in his *Southerner Discovers the South*, and during World War II became Roosevelt's assistant and handled race relations.[6]

The poverty of the South horrified Roosevelt, and he advocated modernization to alleviate it. At Warm Springs he experimented with crop diversification and cattle breeding to demonstrate how farmers could break out of the cotton economy. As for blacks, it never occurred to him to question white supremacy, but being humane, he favored better education and an improved livelihood for them as well as whites.

The deficiencies that bothered Roosevelt the most were of minor concern to some of the dominant Democrats of the South, but in the end they would give them trouble. Here are some that Roosevelt talked about:

There was the exorbitant cost of electricity. Georgia Power contributed to the polio program at Warm Springs, as its president ruefully reminded Roosevelt in the late thirties. But Georgia Power charged such high rates that kerosene lamps lit the farmhouses in the area. The whistle of the train in the night reminded Roosevelt that it was bringing South from Wisconsin the milk that Georgia itself should be producing. And there was the deplorable state of education. The nineteen-year-old principal of the local elementary school had finished only his freshman year at Athens, and was earning four hundred dollars a year. Both in education and salary he was far in advance of his staff of three teachers.[7]

Roosevelt as president, always mindful of maintaining his southern power base, and dependent upon the southern committee chairmen in Congress, was cautious but also restless, intermittently pushing for new programs. They would redress shortcomings that worried him, but sometimes they would also undermine dogmas even he had not seemed to question.

The problems were apparent only later. During the campaign

of 1932 Roosevelt was optimistic in a time of deep pessimism, and he was sufficiently vague to keep intact a broad coalition from well to the left to well to the right, united in their rejection of Hoover. He campaigned through the South, although he could count upon carrying every state, in order to build popular support for the future. During the interregnum in 1932–33, he continued to be bland, not proposing programs against which opposition could rally, and giving the southern leadership in Congress the false impression that they, not the president, would be the decisive factor in a New Deal. The single prospective piece of legislation he announced in advance was the Tennessee Valley Authority, which he was ready to enlarge from the long-sought production of low-cost power and fertilizer into a great experiment in southern regional planning based on local committees—"grass roots democracy." This bold proposal was attractive to all southern leaders, but attracted relatively little attention amidst the growing alarm over bank closings.

The solemn, firm way in which Roosevelt promised strong, decisive action in his first inaugural address, at the height of the banking crisis, ended permanently any notion that he would be a weak president in the tutelage of Congress. The surge of public opinion in his support was so strong and emotional that at first few of the southern congressional leaders dared openly oppose him. Marvin Jones of Texas, chairman of the House agriculture committee, would not sponsor the bill to establish the AAA, which went well beyond what he had sought, but in the end Jones did no more than help add some constructive amendments. By May 1933, Congress was already playing a considerable part in the shaping of legislation, but except for the unreconstructed Senator Carter Glass of Virginia and a very few others, the southerners, whatever their personal misgivings, were riding the popular New Deal tide. Part of what carried them along was the enthusiasm of their constituents, and part the fact that the canny Roosevelt, like Wilson in 1913, did not distribute patronage until he had obtained his program. The desper-

ate state of the economy in the spring of 1933, continuing down-
ward until May, both generated the southern enthusiasm for a
president who promised some quick aid, and intensified the
pressure upon southern congressmen to produce federal jobs for
their lieutenants. And, in any event, southern conservatives and
liberals alike rejoiced that through the relief and agricultural
programs and TVA, federal money was coming into the South.

There is a more important parallel to Wilson worth noting.
Roosevelt also worked with the Democratic congressional dele-
gations in power. These were the regulars, some of them, like
Senator Josiah Bailey of North Carolina, still addicted to the
rhetoric and thought patterns of the "lost cause," a few, of course,
like Senator Hugo Black of Alabama, were on some issues to the
left of the president. Even less than Wilson could Roosevelt
spare the time or the political effort to build organizations whose
prime loyalty was to him. At the beginning of his campaign he
had made the crucial, and quite wise, decision to work with the
existing state organizations—even those who had opposed him
for the nomination—rather than outsiders who had organized
Roosevelt clubs. Out of these state organizations had come the
members of both houses of Congress, and to them went most of
the appointments. They continued strong, and, for the most part,
rather conservative, throughout the New Deal.

There were exceptions. The Women's Division of the Democratic National Committee had labored energetically and fruit-
fully during the campaign. By dint of much effort, its head, Molly
Dewson, together with Eleanor Roosevelt and Frances Perkins,
the new secretary of labor, managed to obtain a number of appointments despite the stiff resistance of the organizations. There
was, for example, Sue Shelton White of Tennessee, a former
women's suffrage leader, who served on the Consumers' Advisory Board of the NRA, and helped lay the foundations of the Social
Security system.[8]

Other exceptions came in the relief programs under the supervision of Harry Hopkins who in his first years as a New Dealer

outraged the organizations by his disregard for politics. The rise of Aubrey Williams, originally from Alabama, to become his chief assistant and later the head of the National Youth Administration, was not to be credited to political organizations. Late in the New Deal thanks to Williams's indiscretions, they managed to get rid of him. Sometimes there were surprises. The arch-conservative Senator "Cotton Ed" Smith of South Carolina obtained an appointment for a young economist, son of one of the largest, most influential cotton planters in the state. Soon the economist became the prime assistant to the most powerful and advanced of the northern New Deal senators, Robert Wagner, and was drafting labor and social legislation that was anathema to the southerners. I am referring to Leon Keyserling, who was to become the chairman of President Truman's Council of Economic Advisers.[9]

A large number of southern appointees to New Deal organizations received their positions for political reasons rather than conspicuous administrative talents or social philosophy. A place had to be found for Theodore G. Bilbo, that important enemy of Huey Long's, a blatant demagogue, but an advocate of New Deal programs, who in 1932 had completed a term as governor of Mississippi. Roosevelt dumped him on the AAA, which placed him in charge of its press clippings—gaining for him the unofficial title of "pastemaster general." In 1934, he won election to the Senate.

All sorts of southerners had a hand in New Deal administration. Most of them, especially in state and local supervision of relief and agricultural programs, owed their positions to the party hierarchy. They were of varying backgrounds and talents, not easily assigned to one or another school of thought during the early New Deal before firm liberal-conservative battle lines had been drawn. Some evolved surprisingly in their thinking and responsibilities.

While one of Hopkins's prime assistants in relief administration was Aubrey Williams, a minister turned social work execu-

tive; another assistant, also an Alabaman, was Thad Holt, Birmingham businessman, who had been president of the Junior
Chamber of Commerce, and active in civic enterprises. Holt's
experiences in the depression and New Deal are illustrative of
the evolving problem of economic rehabilitation in the South. In
the 1920s Governor "Bibb the Builder" Graves appointed Holt to
become the first director and organizer of the Alabama Industrial
Development Board, to bring new plants into the state. "We
were attempting to encourage industrial employment in Alabama," Holt has said, "and to move some of the people off the
farms into the industries, better pay and so forth."

When the Great Depression made that enterprise futile, President Hoover organized the President's Emergency Committee for
Employment to stimulate volunteer efforts to create jobs. Graves
again turned to Holt, who encouraged industries, municipalities,
and counties to establish work relief projects. Since there was not
the money in Alabama to fund the projects, Holt sought it in
Washington. President Hoover, Holt was told, was insisting,
"We will not dip into the Federal Treasury," but in 1932 finally
authorized the Reconstruction Finance Corporation to make
loans to states. Holt headed the RFC program for the southeast,
then became director of the Alabama Relief Administration, established before Roosevelt was inaugurated. With other state
administrators he was summoned to Washington in the fall of
1933 to hear Hopkins announce the launching of the Civil Works
Administration:

> At first they could not believe what they were hearing: the
> Federal Government putting needy people [to] work on
> locally-sponsored public projects with wages paid by a U.S.
> Treasury Disbursing Officer. In fact, neither could the Presi-
> dent of the University of Alabama, who was carrying around in
> his pocket some $250,000 in "worthless" state warrants. [He]
> couldn't believe he could build a dining hall in his women's
> dormitory and not have to pay it back.

The jobs and the public improvements that work relief brought
in Alabama received acclaim, but not everyone was pleased by

the innovations. "I got away with what some people politically called murder," Holt has reminisced, "when [for] the first time in the history of Alabama I believe, . . . blacks working on a county road were paid exactly the same amount as whites." The going wage for road work was so low that Holt received a postcard from a worker in Geneva County asking if it was fair for him to have to walk two miles to the job, work ten hours, then walk two miles back, for fifty cents a day. Generally the pay had been a dollar a day for whites, and lower for blacks. The work relief program raised the wage to thirty cents an hour.

As for Holt, he can cite with satisfaction the millions of dollars that the federal relief programs brought into the state, the employment they created through the FERA, the CWA, the CCC, and the NYA, and the aid that the agricultural programs provided. He enjoyed the support of Aubrey Williams whom he first met when Williams was regional representative for the FERA. It was Williams, "accused of being very radical," who sponsored Holt in Alabama and brought him to Washington to be an assistant administrator of the WPA. Thereafter Holt was once again a civic and business leader in Birmingham.[10]

The transit of Holt in four years from seeking to lure industry into Alabama to decreeing thirty cents an hour pay for white and blacks alike working on roads, is indicative of the rapid changes the depression and New Deal brought to the South.

Overall the changes, both economic and social, brought Roosevelt the loyalty of the dispossessed, who made some slight gain even if primarily it was hope. The changes also brought him the wrath and distrust of many of those who had based their lives and thought upon the old order.

For the South, as throughout the nation, the New Deal recovery program was a bootstrap scheme in which the agricultural and industrial schemes were to operate without heavy federal appropriations behind the protective barrier of the Republican Hawley-Smoot Tariff. As a sop to southern ideological sensitivities, and to promote Latin American trade, Roosevelt did accept Secretary of State Cordell Hull's reciprocal trade program.

What was important in the New Deal recovery program was to bolster the price of cotton, tobacco, and other basic commodities through one or another crop restriction device, without letting the world's cheap surplus pour in. The price of cotton did go up. As is well known, landowners received much of the return, and renters and sharecroppers very little. Not at all as Roosevelt or Secretary of Agriculture Wallace had intended, the program even led to evicting of tenants and the hiring of relatively small numbers of hands. The era of the huge tractor and gang-plow had already arrived, and the mechanical cotton picker was in an experimental stage. The AAA hastened what was inevitable, partly through loopholes in the legislation, partly because the county AAA committees seldom represented other than the landowners.

The NRA and subsequent schemes to raise both the prices of manufactured goods and the wages of laborers, hit hard at an area where the major attraction for outside industry was lower wages, and the assurance that union organizers need not be feared. Mills with outmoded machinery, competing only through their lower wages and longer hours were especially hard hit. Marginal workers in factories, and even the black retainers who ran errands for retail merchants, were victims of the NRA. When the NRA code-making process began, southern textile mill owners tried immediately to win recognition of the traditional southern differential—submitting a budget for workers in which coffee was a rare luxury. They gained only part of what they wanted. The effort to win new industries continued, with the conventional promises of cheap, dependable labor, low or no taxes for years, and all the rest. (The *Wall Street Journal* for September 21, 1983 contained exactly such an advertisement, but with the locale just across the California border in Mexicali, Mexico—such is the competition the South faces today.) Ingenious Mississippi promoters were even able to incorporate New Deal largesse in their schemes. Five communities built so-called "industrial training

schools" with WPA funds and made them available to industrialists who had moved from the North. Girls worked without
wages for six to twelve weeks, then at learner's wages; their
supervisors sometimes became "instructors" receiving their pay
from the Office of Education. One need only add that in efforts to
protect the wage differential there was energetic resistance to the
National Labor Relations Act, the Social Security Act, and the
Fair Labor Standards Act. Yet these pieces of legislation did go
through with many southern votes in Congress cast for them.
Living standards did edge upwards.

Altogether considerable money moved into the South during
the depression, helping improve conditions there, not only
through relief projects and crop benefits, but also the building of
TVA dams and transmission lines, and other public works. A
number of New Deal agencies eased credit. Income payments in
the South by 1940 were, thanks to the federal government, 1
percent above the 1929 level, George Tindall points out. In the
rest of the nation they were still 10 percent below 1929 figures.
Southern incomes were still far below the national average, but
close to that of Canada, and high by world standards. They were
to soar far higher in World War II and after. [11]

Recovery, although by no means at a satisfactory level, had
come to the South, it can be argued, and it had come largely
through federal expenditures. Yet southern leaders from 1934 on
were pressuring Roosevelt to cut the budget. John Nance Garner
informed Roosevelt in June 1937, "Texas never in its history was
in better shape, economically and in every other way, than it is at
the present time," and added that people were asking when the
budget was going to be balanced. This was Garner's reply to data
Roosevelt sent him indicating that 336,200 people were receiving
federal aid in Texas. [12]

In the late 1930s, southern Senators under the able leadership
of Pat Harrison of Mississippi fought year after year to slash New
Deal requests. There were exceptions, of course. Harrison did
seek to obtain federal aid to education, which Mississippi and

other southern states badly needed. Senator John Bankhead of
Alabama supported the Harrison bill with "the very greatest reluctance because I am quite certain . . . that . . . the race
question will be injected." Roosevelt did not favor the bill because he was more concerned with obtaining money for relief,
and the pressure upon him was great to do more for northern
cities.[13]

Gradually, the long-standing cordiality between Roosevelt and
the southern leaders wore down to superficial pleasantries. Most
of these leaders, like Senator Harrison, concerned about the
quality of education, and Senator Bankhead and Representative
Marvin Jones, the sponsors of legislation to aid tenant farmers,
wanted in one or another way to improve the southern way of
life. But above all, they were worried because the New Deal
seemed to be taking them too fast and building a staggering
national debt. Their most powerful supporters and generous
campaign contributors were afraid of changes that would affect
their businesses. That was true even of base-pointing. In the
early New Deal, the inequity of charging a Pittsburgh base-point
price for Birmingham steel was modified. In October 1936 when
an anti-base-point clause was inserted in the Robinson-Patman
bill, Representative Fred M. Vinson of Kentucky in cooperation
with Speaker William B. Bankhead, "made quick contact with
the representatives of all the cotton districts, the sugar districts
[and others] . . . that would be severely affected by such drastic
legislation," and persuaded the sponsors of the bill to move to
strike out the paragraph. Even more serious was their concern
that the New Deal might erode white supremacy. At the outset
of the New Deal, the political leaders seemed to have the president's ear. Now he seemed more responsive to northern administrators they considered radicals, like Harry Hopkins, and to
southerners like Aubrey Williams, who was making the NYA educational programs available to blacks as well as whites. Other
southern administrators were more careful to abide by tradition.
Robert Fechner kept the CCC not only segregated, but almost out
of reach for southern blacks.[14]

Undoubtedly Roosevelt was shifting, as suggested by his second inaugural's emphasis upon the underprivileged one-third, toward an increasing concern with poverty and injustice. Much of his focus was upon the South. Eleanor Roosevelt, who was continually keeping her husband informed of conditions she had seen, was a formidable influence. So too were many southern reformers working for New Deal agencies, and some of the emerging politicians like Claude Pepper of Florida and the Texans Maury Maverick and Lyndon Johnson.

In the spring of 1938 when Pepper, an ardent New Dealer, won the Democratic primary in Florida, Roosevelt was encouraged to undertake a "purge" in the primaries of some of the most stalwart conservatives who had fought his Supreme Court bill and other pieces of major legislation.

The great manifesto of the "purge" was the National Emergency Council's *Report on Economic Conditions of the South*. Clark Foreman, a white Atlantan, who handled racial policies for Secretary of the Interior Harold L. Ickes, persuaded Roosevelt to authorize what in effect was the southern reformers' manifesto for change. Despite its title, it was less a sober economic report than a political document which Roosevelt cited as reason for electing New Dealers to Congress. Yet it was a distinctly southern product. Neither Howard Odum nor Rupert Vance served on the advisory committee, but the *Report*, only sixty-four pages long was a detailed, systematic setting forth of facts in the fashion for which they were renowned, incorporating much of their material. Southerners had drafted each of the fifteen sections, federal departments and agencies had supplied the data, and the Central Statistical Board had checked the figures. From beginning to end the facts were appalling, but what most stung southern pride was Roosevelt's covering statement:

> The South presents right now the Nation's No. 1 economic problem—the Nation's problem, not merely the South's. For we have an economic unbalance in the Nation as a whole, due to this very condition of the South.[15]

Because Roosevelt could find only weak candidates to support against prestigious senators like Walter George of Georgia and Millard Tydings of Maryland, who had effective organizations behind them, the "purge" was a fiasco. Yet public opinion polls indicated that in the South as elsewhere in the nation, Roosevelt's popularity remained little diminished. He had become and he remained the hero of those millions of southerners in distress who had been desperate for aid. Some had rallied around Huey Long who promised them much, but as Alan Brinkley has shown, their support of Long did not necessarily mean their rejection of Roosevelt. A Louisiana woman once told me that on a wall in her household when she was a child, there was a madonna between two portraits—of Long and Roosevelt. Too much can be made of the failure of the purge. It was one step in the escalation of Roosevelt's long-standing contention with conservatives that led toward the Dixiecrat movement of 1948, but it did not signify a popular rejection of him.

Although the Munich crisis in September 1938 and the events that followed forced Roosevelt to direct much of his attention thereafter to defense policy, he continued to press Congress for aid to the dispossessed—which could mean much to those in the South. Congress continued to pare down or block entirely his proposals. Even if there had been no foreign problems, there would have been no new program larger than those already in effect to raise southern living standards. Roosevelt's relations with the southerners in Congress continued much the same, except that when defense became urgent several of those like Carter Glass, who had been most critical of his domestic policies, came to his aid on foreign policy and military matters. The building of army camps and defense plants in the South brought the massive spending that Congress had previously opposed.

Despite conservative opposition, social change came in the South as a result of the New Deal. There had been some alleviation of the worst poverty. There had been some experimentation with agricultural improvements; contour plowing to curb soil erosion has had an enduring effect. There was much controversy

concerning the Resettlement Administration and the Farm Security Administration, and much went wrong in the planning and
execution of community projects, but they did provide better
housing and sometimes a livelihood for some thousands of people. The TVA, generating cheap power, and the REA delivering it
in the countryside, brought electricity to farms and stimulated
industry. Relief monies brought improvements in education, and
the WPA brought federal arts, theatre, and music projects. The
Writers' Project gathered much southern folklore, oral tradition,
and reminiscence—as witness the account of former slaves and
collections like *These Are Our Lives*. In most of these activities,
blacks shared as well as whites. And those blacks who had moved
North and were voting, were bringing pressure upon the
Roosevelt administration for civil rights. They were not very
successful until 1941 when they threatened a march on Washington, which led to the establishment of the Fair Employment
Practices Commission.[16]

More interesting than catalogs of programs are the changes
that the depression and the New Deal were bringing about
among potential leaders of the South. Through the 1920s, Virginia Durr, who grew up on the outskirts of Montgomery, Alabama, had been, she says a conformist, the vice-president of the
Junior League, and not aware of southern poverty until the depression:

> Have you even seen a child with rickets? Shaking as with
> palsy. No proteins, no milk. And the companies pouring milk
> into gutters. . . .
> It was the first time I had seen the other side of the tracks.
> The rickets, the pellagra—it shook me up. I saw the world as it
> really was.

Virginia Durr persuaded the dairy to open milk dispensaries
by arguing, "If these people got a taste of milk, they might get in
the habit of buying it—when they got jobs." By the end of the
New Deal she was organizing southern women to fight against
the poll tax.[17]

Throughout the South, as in the rest of the nation, the New

Deal was training those who in the future worked for its idealistic goals. Lady Bird Johnson recalls the "busy and wonderful year" when her husband, Lyndon B. Johnson, headed the National Youth Administration in Texas. "Lyndon learned a lot and made friends that lasted all his life." A generation later when the Johnsons came back to dedicate a job-training corps at San Marcos, Texas, she looked about the platform. "There was a judge who handled the guest of honor, the governor, and on up to the President. All of them had been with the National Youth Administration. . . . So it was a breeding ground for learning and achievement." Quite a few of these New Dealers went on to Washington, as did Lyndon Johnson in 1937 when he was elected to Congress.

> It was a yeasty, exciting time, Mrs. Johnson remembers, and the people really felt they could roll up their sleeves and make America great. Lyndon had an expression about that. '"You feel like charging Hell with a bucket of water.'" There were very few times in our country's life when so many good minds gathered together in that city intent on raising the level of living and the safety of the American people. I'm so glad I got to be a part of it.[18]

The New Deal,
Southern Agriculture,
and Economic Change

PETE DANIEL

Patrician newspaperman and author Virginius Dabney recalled
that during Franklin D. Roosevelt's first term as president a
friend of his "counted the number of separate Federal agencies
which were trying to help the farmer in one Southern county,
and reported finding no fewer than twenty-seven!"[1] Dabney's
exclamation point suggested a radical break with the past. Indeed, the South's tradition of opposition to federal intrusion
dated at least to the debate over federal assumption of Revolutionary War debts and reemerged time and again—with the Old
Republicans, the nullification crisis, the Civil War, and insistence that states could best handle race relations after Emancipation. To accept, indeed, welcome, dozens of federal agencies
signaled a shift in the relationship of southern states to the federal government. There was an apocalyptic aspect to this change.
To a people who still tasted defeat, dimly recalled a promise of a
yeoman's paradise, and believed in Biblical redemption, the
New Deal appeared as the millennium; and its personification,
Franklin D. Roosevelt, sent the twenty-seven federal agencies to
revitalize the economy, punish the unrighteous, and usher in a
reign of justice, or so it seemed. What at first appears as an
inexplicable acceptance of federal agencies among a people who
had been largely shielded from national aid can be better understood by examining briefly the nature of southern communities

37

and some of the forces of change in the half-century before the
New Deal.

I

Southern states not only repudiated federal intrusion but in
many respects shunned government aid from any source. Southern counties, towns, and communities handled their problems
informally. Until the second quarter of the twentieth century,
state and local governments in the rural South had provided
meager organized relief. Although there were people who lived
on the edge of survival, southern communities informally looked
after their own. In the largely agrarian southern society, even
uneducated and unskilled people could find enough work to put
food on the table. The work ethic permeated the South, and for
those who did not work the community had pillorying terms—
lazy, good for nothing, no account, trash. Even the most dismal
tenant farmer took pride in working, and his wife likely took
pride in her kitchen, children, and chores. The South measured
its people by brawn and stoicism, although the ability to tell
stories and church attendance, or the lack of it, also figured.
Those who accepted the gospel of hard work received community
support even if they failed, but the community scorned the idle.

The Good Book after all encouraged extending a helping hand
to those who faltered, for it observed that the poor would always
be present. Even a dedicated beggar enjoyed community approval as William Faulkner revealed in his novel, *The Town*. Old
Het, a black beggarwoman, relied on the scriptures for justifying
her calling. "There's some folks thinks all I does, I tromps this
town all day long from can-see to cant, with a hand full of gimme
and a mouth full of much oblige. They're wrong. I serves Jefferson too. If it's more blessed to give than to receive like the Book
say, this town is blessed to a fare-you-well because it's steady full
of folks willing to give anything from a nickel up to a old hat. But
I'm the onliest one I knows that steady receives. So how is Jeffer-

son going to be steady blessed without me steady willing from
dust-dawn to dust-dark, rain or snow or sun, to say much
oblige?"[2]

Southern rural and small town communities were a kaleido-
scope of relationships among blacks and whites, men and
women, rich and poor, old and young, farmers and merchants,
lenders and borrowers. In the cracks between the crystals, there
was room for nonconformity, but there also lingered the threat of
ostracism or violence if the established patterns were threatened.
The strength of communities had helped rural southerners to
withstand the forces that since the Civil War had reconfigured
the tenure system and driven many people into dependency
upon landlords for the elements of survival.

As Civil War and Reconstruction memories retreated into the
mists of fantasy, landownership concentrated into fewer hands,
and a new set of owners—life insurance companies, banks, mort-
gage companies, or counterparts of the local Snopes family—took
title to the land. Prolific southerners filled the countryside, and
farmers increasingly found it difficult to find good land to till. At
the same time, the position of the cotton-growing states east of
the Mississippi River was weakened by the boll weevil infestation
that began in Texas in the 1890s and by 1920 had reached the
Atlantic Ocean. The weevil not only destroyed cotton and scattered farmers as it advanced but it also increased the cost of
production due to the poison and intensive cultivation methods
needed to halt its life-cycle. The pace of cotton's westward migration—its destiny—accelerated, and the Mississippi Delta,
Oklahoma, Texas, and later New Mexico and California, which
had less infestation and thus a lower cost of production, out-
produced the old cotton growing states of the East. The disruption of World War I, especially the migration of blacks, the collapse of the agricultural market in 1920, the lack of any plan
successfully to reduce the growing surplus of commodities, the
1927 Mississippi River flood, the drought three years later, and
the depression came as successive jolts to rural southerners. To a

people who read their Bibles, the hard times suggested some divine retribution. Such a combination of economic and climatic disasters had never coincided before, and the remedy was beyond the means of communities, a strain on state governments, and ideologically repugnant to the federal government dominated by Republicans.[3]

II

In the context of these troubles, Roosevelt loomed as a prophetic figure, a Moses who could unseat the entrenched powers that held people in bondage. Farmers listened to his fireside chats, placed his photograph on the mantel, wrote him letters, cheered the unprecedented activity of Congress in translating his ideas into policy, and welcomed the host of agencies that suddenly materialized in every community. As so many letters and reports revealed, southern people were impressed with such agencies, because no one had ever shown any such interest in their welfare. For example, Sarah and John Easton lived in an abandoned filling station in rural Wilson County, North Carolina. "I'm a Democrat; I stand for the New Deal and Roosevelt," John Easton told two WPA interviewers. "I am for the WPA, the NYA, the NRA, the AAA, the FHA, and crop control. . . . We've got mighty little of the government money," he admitted, but "the government shore give us enough when it paid for Amy's leg operation." One of his twin daughters had been born with a deformity that had been corrected with the help of a federal agency.[4] Such stories were replicated throughout the South as millions of people had been touched to a lesser or greater extent by some federal agency. Yet the impact upon people varied, and it depended on race, class, commodity culture, local and federal administrators, and many other factors.

When the federal government set up work and relief programs that substituted for sharecropping or community alms, most recipients were elated. Such aid did not, at least at first, have the debilitating effect of the English Poor Laws a century before.[5] Government jobs in many cases paid more than rural people had ever earned. So long as federal relief policies did not disperse the seasonal work force or drive wages too high planters accepted them.

Historians who have studied the rural South of the 1930s have shown that some of the New Deal agencies were insensitive to the human disruption in cotton-growing areas, especially in Arkansas where the Southern Tenant Farmers Union emerged. These tenants basically wanted to preserve and reform the sharecropping system, as did their champions in the Cotton Section who were purged for defending them. While some early New Deal agencies offered innovative approaches to jobs and housing, others created after the initial mood of experimentation had passed represented the status quo or advocated reform of longstanding abuses in the tenant system.[6] On the other hand, the AAA and the USDA in general epitomized the forces of change that insisted on clearing off surplus farmers and instituting a more businesslike system of farming. The government represented larger farmers who, like business interests thirty yeras earlier, were attempting to rationalize agriculture. To find the most revolutionary aspects of the New Deal in the South, one must look not to the welfare programs that pacified the dispossessed or the trickle of dollars that spilled into the pockets of sharecroppers and tenants but rather to the changing structure of agriculture fueled by the AAA.

In a larger sense, the twenty-seven federal agencies that Virginius Dabney's friend counted substituted for landlords and community relief. The federal government increasingly supplanted landlords and merchants with federal relief, and, at the same time, with acreage allotments and benefit payments assumed direction over agriculture that had once belonged to the planter class. Changes in such responsibilities altered the relationship between landlord and tenant and created a different attitude toward relief. After initial opposition and enduring ambivalence, landlords and merchants abdicated their paternalistic role. More thoroughly than Sherman's army, the New Deal troops marched through the southern countryside and reconfigured it; the old order declined, and in its place emerged a rural South modeled on the long-held dream of the United States Department of Agriculture of large farms, plentiful implements, and scientific farming.

In retrospect it is easy to regard the changes in southern rural life as inevitable, as part of some cosmic design. Was it inevitable that sharecropping disappear, that machines replace people, that surplus rural laborers migrate to become surplus urban laborers, or that farms expand and become more businesslike? If one looks at the Federal Emergency Relief Administration (FERA) program in Franklin County, North Carolina, the answer is no. This county was targeted as a rural problem area, one of the worst of southern counties in terms of unemployment and the need for federal relief. Indeed, four banks failed during the depression, and in 1934 only one remained open. Most rural people were tenants; two-thirds of the county's farmers had no stake in ownership. Although idle sawmills and textile plants contributed to the unemployment problem, the primary problem sprang from the agricultural depression and "the landlord-tenant system having proved inadequate to the task of carrying the labor supply over the present period of restricted production."

The FERA in Franklin County attacked problems with imagination and boldness. When the Civil Works Administration shut down in March 1934 after spending $52,000 and employing 253 people, 807 families faced unemployment. Because so few jobs existed outside agriculture even in good times, FERA administrator C. W. E. Pittman searched for farms. Four hundred relief families secured tenant positions, and one hundred village people sought work relief and odd jobs. Another hundred clients were unemployable and went on direct relief. The other two hundred families could work, but depression shut them out of the traditional farming culture. There was plenty of land available but not enough work stock or tobacco and cotton allotments. The State Emergency Relief Administration furnished the county seventeen mules, and more than any single factor this raised the hopes of people on relief.

The FERA staff called a meeting with an advisory group composed of the county farm agent, agriculture teachers, federal and private lending representatives, and the farm managers from two life insurance companies; each of these brought a landowner to the meeting. All sympathized with the program and offered suggestions. A sharecropping arrangement seemed familiar and promising, so the agency tried to place the two hundred families "on such terms as would permit them to produce more corn, vegetables, peas, and sorghum than they could consume" and barter the surplus "for items they could not produce, namely, meat, flour, and clothing." Pittman's plan turned back the clock to an older tradition of subsistence and barter that preceded commercial agriculture.

The relief families got nowhere with suspicious landlords, for although the government promised support, landowners feared they would end up furnishing relief clients. So case workers and clients together visited landlords, and, despite the scarcity of work stock, placed all families. It became impossible, however, to furnish both fertilizer and supervision, so many clients worked independently. The tenure arrangements varied: 15 clients farmed their own land, 19 paid no rent, 2 cleared land for its use, 2 others worked for the landlord, and 169 sharecropped for one-fourth of the corn and sorghum. Thirty-six families shared FERA mules, 18 used their own, 98 gave one-fourth of the corn and sorghum, 53 exchanged a day's work for the landlord for a day with the mule, and 2 used animals rented by the FERA.

These arrangements produced an average return of $133.23 per family, which, the report argued, "seems a small return for the efforts of six months until it is considered relatively." Had these clients not worked, they would have had no income, but with this stake and the food they raised, many could barter for

other supplies and survive without government aid. "Most people are deeply ingrained with the instinct to exalt work," the
report stressed. By requiring work the program had stifled criticism that originated when the federal government began relief
work. The report concluded optimistically that the success "pre-
pares the way for future progress of these people."

The FERA boasted that the program salvaged the pride of poor
people. Although they were inadequately housed, fed, and doc-
tored, the government program had given them hope. From the
material standpoint the relief work had been successful, but
"from a spiritual standpoint it has yielded a rich harvest in increased hope, self-reliance and confidence." A symbol of this
attitude hung in Pittman's office, for he had obtained a client's
patched shirt. "The shirt was taken from a colored client for
display purposes," the report noted, "not because it was so badly
worn but because of the infinite care that had been taken to keep
it patched." The shirt exemplified the tenancy system that had
been torn and patched so many times as landlords and tenants
bargained for the tattered returns from cash crops. Pittman recognized the amazing resilience in this client and directed the
man's energies to the land. Increasingly federal agencies would
shunt such people to cities and away from all that was familiar
and remunerative.[7]

The Franklin County program revealed how little experienced
farmers needed to succeed in the country. Without growing cotton or tobacco, most of these families came out ahead primarily
because the rehabilitation program gave them hope, and it
supervised them as much as funds permitted. The government in
these cases simply replaced the traditional furnishing system
with impartial and enthusiastic oversight. That these unlikely
candidates succeeded raises questions about the operation of the
old sharecropping system and the exploitation that characterized
it, for even growing cash crops few tenants broke even at settlement time. The FERA program stressed an older form of economic relationships—barter and noncommercial crops. It took

little to survive in depressed Franklin County, but to break out of
the bonds of dependence it did take opportunity. If the FERA
could produce such results, it raises serious questions about the
lost potential of the Extension Service and later of the Resettlement Administration and the Farm Security Administration.

Unfortunately, the Franklin County FERA success was, if not
unique, one of the rare triumphs in southern problem counties.
If there were no jobs outside agriculture, tilling the land offered
the only hope for work for unemployed farmers. As the FERA
attempted to apply emergency aid to farmers, the Agricultural
Adjustment Administration (AAA) worked at cross purposes by
reducing acreage. It did not take long for farmers to figure out
that less acreage under cultivation would mean less tenants doing
the cultivating. While the FERA in Franklin County turned away
from commercial farming to rescue displaced farmers, the AAA
commodity programs reconfigured the relationship between
landlord and tenant ushering in a shift to wage labor and ultimately to mechanization.

The acreage allotment, the amount of a commodity that a
farmer could grow, in most programs went to the landowner, and
this robbed tenants of any bargaining power. In September 1933,
tobacco farmer Maynard P. West of Axton, Virginia, attended a
meeting in Martinsville. Landlords, he warned, would gladly
reduce acreage, but they would also reduce the number of tenants they used proportionately. "I believe it would be just to
allow a tennant to carry his allotment with him from farm to
farm," West suggested, "and require Land lords to reduce their
planting in accordance with the total indicated allotment allowed
them and their tennants." This, he insisted, would give tenants a
bargaining lever and offer protection from eviction. John B. Hutson, chief of the Tobacco Section of the AAA, rejected West's idea
and pointed out that it "would cause landlords to bid for these
tenants in order to increase the acreage of tobacco on their particular farm."[8]

Even if West's idea had been implemented in the flue-cured

tobacco area, small farmers would still bear the brunt of reduc-tion. The AAA Rice Section awarded allotments to whoever farmed the land, regardless of tenure, just as West suggested for tobacco farmers. Still, the rice program generated problems. W. J. Lowe of Iowa, Louisiana, personified the ambivalence of many farmers about government intrusion. On the one hand, he re-sented government programs, but he also tired of carping land-lords in the rice area. He suggested in the spring of 1935 that larger landowners reduce their acreage to help smaller growers. He envisioned a model farm of 640 acres that rotated a 300-acre rice allotment that "will fit one irrigation well, one tractor, six mules, one drill, one binder, one thrashing machine and a regu-lar hired man." Farmers who had more than a 300-acre allotment should be cut until they reached the 300-acre level while smaller farmers should be built up to that figure. "It is no worse for the big farmer to come down to three hundred acres," he argued, "than it is to hold the little farmer in bondage so that he cannot rise to a profitable basis." Lowe resented that small farmers had to work under government programs drafted "by high powered politicians that probably never wore overalls or tilled the soil; especially when they are a thousand miles away running the farmers' business, and whom they have never met personally and discussed their views with." While complaining about how farmers had been "planned, checked, inspected, mortgaged, charged, taxed, denied and red-taped," his suggested program would further regiment rice farmers by government planning. Lowe's idea, however, ran counter to the AAA philosophy that generally favored larger farmers. Years later when reduced allot-ments shook the Louisiana rice area in the mid-1950s, farmers revived Lowe's ideas and suggested that the cuts be graduated according to size, like the income tax.[9]

Both West and Lowe offered constructive ideas on protecting small farmers from the disruption that AAA programs set in mo-tion. Although the AAA ignored the suggestions of both farmers, other forces unique to the commodity culture in both areas protected tenants from displacement. Because of the labor-intensive nature of growing tobacco and the protection given by the Tobacco Section to small growers, no massive displacement took place along tobacco road. The highly mechanized rice culture remained stable because of producer allotments and the prohibitive capital requirements needed to start farming rice.

The AAA cotton program, on the other hand, arrived in the South not only at the same time that the cotton culture haltingly edged toward mechanization, but it also attempted to force the same rules upon farmers with vastly different tenure arrangements in the delta, Black Belt, hills, valleys, and plains. Cotton farmers in Meriwether County, Georgia, had worked out a simple tenure arrangement that seemed to fit the needs of many farmers. Located southwest of Atlanta and only a county away from the Alabama line, the county achieved the dubious distinction of being a FERA problem area. Warm Springs, the most famous part of the county, had developed into a rehabilitation center for polio victims. Franklin D. Roosevelt often visited Warm Springs, attracted by the soothing water that he hoped would restore his legs to strength. He ultimately invested a large part of his personal fortune in the center and set up the Warm Springs Foundation. He enjoyed meeting people in the community and often drove his specially equipped automobile through the countryside, stopping to drink moonshine, watch coon hunts, and discuss everyday problems. He owned a farm in the county and raised livestock and grew some crops. He often described himself as a farmer, both because of the Georgia farm and because of his upbringing in bucolic Hyde Park. If there was one part of rural America that Roosevelt knew, it was Meriwether County. Whether he ever measured his New Deal policies by that county remains problematical, but if he did observe the forces flowing from government programs, he must have taken pause.[10]

Farm tenants comprised 75 percent of the 2,430 farm operators in the county, but census categories did not reveal a unique rental plan that characterized the county. Hidden among "other tenants" and even sharecroppers and renters, a substantial number of farmers paid a bale of cotton per plow in rent. Census takers did not record this class separately, but FERA officials estimated that from one-third to two-thirds of all farm tenants were bale-per-plow renters who cultivated about ten acres per plow and produced some four to five bales of cotton. One bale paid for fertilizer, one went to the landlord, and the two or three remaining plus the seed went to the renter. While the 40 percent acreage reduction affected most tenants in the cotton South, it devastated the bale-per-plow arrangement in Meriwether County. Under the AAA, one plow turned only five or six acres after allotment cuts, producing about two-and-a-half bales. After paying the landlord and settling for fertilizer, the renter would only have one-half bale left for his profit and would have been better off without a New Deal.

For example, when cotton sold for 8¢ a pound, a farmer stood to make from $80 to $120 on his two or three bales, and he also got about $75 seed money from five bales. Thus, a renter would earn from $155 to $195 a year per plow under the old arrangement. Under the AAA, with one-half bale that sold for 12¢, he earned $30 for the lint and $45 for the seed from two-and-a-half bales. His yearly earnings came to $75. Of course he got from $4 to $5 per acre for renting the other land to the government, but his yearly earnings did not reach $100. Even if the price of cotton had fallen to 6¢ a pound the renter would have earned from $135 to $165 under the old system.[11]

While the AAA may have worked well in other areas of the South where landlords were fair with payments to tenants, the tenure system in much of Meriwether County turned into chaos. In this sense, the county served as a model, for throughout the South the standard formulas of the AAA seldom took local customs

N.D. prepared the way for large scale farming

into consideration. Instead of rebuilding the South, ushering in a reign of justice and prosperity, or even putting more money into the hands of farmers, the New Deal in many ways destroyed the old structure and prepared the way for large scale farming.

Such standardized federal formulas not only threatened traditional tenure arrangements but also challenged marketing practices in some areas. Farmers of fire-cured tobacco in western Tennessee and Kentucky, for example, sometimes sold their crops directly to local tobacco manufacturers and not at the auction warehouses. The suggested National Recovery Administration code dictated that all tobacco be sold in warehouses, and this provoked outrage and petitions from farmers of fire-cured tobacco. "It is notorious," the petition charged, that on warehouse floors "two baskets may be side by side, of exactly similar quality and sometimes out of the same crop, and one bringing sometimes twice what the other does." The petitioners preferred to sell their tobacco directly "to buyers we know and in whom we have confidence, and selling to them, without taking the uncertainties of the sale on the loose floors, and without paying heavy commissions, etc., to parties selling our tobacco, at less prices, often than we can get for it." In the flue-cured area, where all tobacco was sold in warehouses, warehousemen were complaining about government meddling. Those who warehoused the fire-cured tobacco, on the other hand, welcomed federal intervention.[12]

Some farmers expressed strong contempt for Roosevelt and, at least until forced to by law, refused to go along with acreage reduction. According to Nick Tosches's biography of singer Jerry Lee Lewis, Lewis's father Elmo rented land from Lee Calhoun, a wealthy relative, and he told Elmo "to pay no mind to that damn-fool New Deal cripple talking at people from out of a damn-fool radio." The president had taken the country off the gold standard, Calhoun complained, "but now the fireside-talking fool had gone too far, trying to take us off the dirt standard." So Elmo Lewis did not plow up any cotton in 1933. He took the earnings and bought every Jimmie Rodgers record ever made, got drunk, and sang along with the records. It took standardization with teeth to corral such a spirit.[13]

III

As some of the foregoing examples suggest, analyzing the impact of AAA commodity programs throughout the South presents the historian with a complex set of problems. Each commodity program reflected the ideology of the administrator as well as the statutes. The Cotton Section's Cully Cobb unabashedly represented the planter class, and his rulings consistently came down on their side. As most students of the rural South know, after government payments reached landlords, an indeterminate amount trickled down to tenants. The attempts of the Southern Tenant Farmers Union to rectify this and other injustices have been recorded by several historians and participants. Cobb allowed landlords to evict unneeded tenants, turned his head at many abuses, set up an investigative arm that passed most problems back to local committees that were composed of the very landlords that dominated local affairs, and fired section employees who insisted on interpreting the terms of the contracts favorably to tenants. With acreage cut by some 40 percent, landlords evicted some tenants, changed the status of others to wage hands, and consolidated their operations.

I will offer only one example of how this program benefitted the landowning class. In 1935 the AAA surveyed three plantations in Arkansas to assess the impact of the New Deal. Each planter took a different course in adjusting his tenant population, but all streamlined the work force and used more wage labor than formerly. The report observed that sharecroppers were able to pay off their debts by 1934 and credited it to the benefit of the AAA. Yet the AAA had an even greater impact on the income of the landlord on one of the plantations. While the tenants' share of cotton lint rose from $16,000 in 1932 to $17,000 in 1934, the

history by the #s shows much landlords gotten, did much

landlord's share rose from $39,000 to $77,000 over the same years. Tenants shared more returns from cottonseed over the three years, increasing from $3,000 to $5,000, but the landlord's share rose from $7,000 to $20,000. From all products sold from the plantation, the tenants' share rose from $22,000 to $30,000 while the landlord's share rose from $52,000 to $102,000.[14]

The flue-cured tobacco program under the direction of John B. Hutson furnished a sharp contrast to the Cotton Section. The tenant problem had been eased in part by the flight of many tobacco farmers from the land before the New Deal began. When markets opened in 1933, prices lagged at about ten or eleven cents per pound. Hutson forged a settlement with the tobacco companies to raise prices to a parity level of seventeen cents in exchange for a reduction in acreage the next year. He also protected small growers with a minimum acreage allotment and constantly finetuned the program to make it popular with all classes of farmers. By 1934 farmers of flue-cured tobacco had become addicted to the federal tonic and, except for the 1939 crop year, voted for federal controls at every opportunity. Tobacco, of course, was an extremely labor-intensive crop, and any hope of mechanization lay far into the future. The restructuring that progressed in some cotton areas due to tractors and later harvesters only reached tobacco road in the 1960s. A well-run and popular program and an antiquated work culture combined to preserve traditional relationships in the flue-cured tobacco area.[15]

In contrast to these programs that on the one hand reconfigured the cotton culture and on the other preserved the tobacco culture, the rice program provided an instance of unnecessary federal meddling. First run by A. J. S. Weaver and then by Charles G. Miller, the rice program in 1934 experimented with a complicated marketing agreement between millers and the government and in 1935 turned to a processing tax. Because of the highly mechanized and capital-intensive nature of the prairie rice culture that prohibited rapid expansion, such controls were for the most part unnecessary; they were certainly ineffective. There is little reason to believe that the rice program had much effect on production or provided orderly marketing of the crop. The most innovative feature of the program proved the allotment policy. The Rice Section awarded allotments not to landowners only but also to producers, regardless of tenure, just as tobacco farmer Maynard P. West had suggested for his neighbors. Thus, a rice tenant could take his hip-pocket allotment with him and bargain with a landlord for terms.[16] Such a policy, had it been utilized by cotton and tobacco administrators, could have drastically altered the configuration of these rural work cultures.

By the mid-1930s, millions of southerners had tasted the New Deal tonic, and many had become addicted. The small doses of federal money and jobs blurred a central issue—what would become of farming as they had known it? Huey Long, senator from Louisiana, was skeptical of the New Deal and offered his own patent medicine. In a 1935 radio address, punctuated by the jingle "Every Man a King," Long charged that five million more Americans were on the dole than during the previous year and that one million more were unemployed. In rural areas, he charged, crop reduction had led to idleness and unemployment, but at the same time people were starving. He would allow farmers to grow as much as they wanted, and when a year's supply accumulated, farmers could take off a year, labor on public works projects, or attend school. He charged that the frenzied New Deal activity clouded the conservative nature of most programs. The New Deal, he joked in another broadcast, was like St. Vitus's Dance. Whatever the failings of Long's analysis, he understood that rural people had not benefitted all that much from the New Deal and that it was disrupting traditional farming patterns.[17]

Yet rural people supported the New Deal, and ironically, those who profited least supported the president most faithfully. Part of this enigma can be explained by the fact that many people did profit from the New Deal, and even those who received only

Hope accounts for those who profitted most, less supporting ESD R. tlp [handwritten annotation]

crumbs dreamed of other programs that they might qualify for. They also received a barrage of propaganda from New Deal spokesmen on the radio. Roosevelt's fireside chats were incredibly effective in boosting morale and claiming successes. The First Lady, several of her children, political advisor Louis Howe, cabinet members, and representatives from every agency explained the cornucopia of benefits bursting from Washington. Soap operas, moreover, allowed escape. The radio proved a magical agent of consensus, raising hopes and muting protest.[18]

The benefit payments to landowners provide a clear example of the bias in New Deal rural aid. Having written elsewhere of the direction of government payments to large landowners, I will only reiterate my conclusions and tailor them to the three commodities that I discussed previously. The primary source for analyzing government payments to large corporations, a Senate report, only listed either those who received $10,000 or more from the government or firms that had 150 or more farms under contract. It only revealed the tip of the landowner pyramid.

In Leflore County, Mississippi, for example, two cotton plantations received nearly $23,000 in 1934. Since county farmers received $262,200 in AAA payments, these two plantations got almost 9 percent of the county payments. It is problematical how much of this trickled down to tenants. In the case of the Mississippi State Penitentiary in Sunflower County, no doubt the state retained all $155,000 received over the three-year period.

Only one insurance company appeared on the schedule of owners receiving $10,000 or more, yet these companies dominated the list of multiple landowners that reported 150 or more farms under AAA contracts. Connecticut General Life Insurance Company from its Washington County holdings in 1934 received $35,000 and in 1935 $32,000. The firm had 179 cotton farms under AAA contract in 1934–35, yet it was not the largest holder of cotton farms by far. John Hancock Mutual Life Insurance Company listed 1,580 farms under cotton contracts, Metropolitan 1,141, Prudential 999, Aetna 705, Travelers 636, Union Central 609, General American 602, and several other companies had hundreds of farms. In all, fifty-five multiple landowners who reported 150 or more AAA contracts owned 10,858 cotton farms.

  Most payments went to growers in the western areas of the cotton belt. Indeed, North Carolina and Georgia only appeared on the 1933 list, South Carolina did not have a planter who qualified, Louisiana remained on it two years and received $413,000, and Alabama planters only got $130,000 over the three years. In contrast, Mississippi landowners received $2.5 million, Arkansas $2.1 million, and Texas $1.2 million. This analysis, of course, omits the second tier of owners who were also large operators. Perhaps the most significant aspect of the report was the revelation that some $7 million of AAA money went not to struggling farmers but to large corporations and landlords.[19] In this respect, the New Deal propped up business interests and commercial farmers.

Because of the small size of tobacco farms, the Senate report revealed only two landowners that fell into the large categories. A Georgia farmer received $11,000, and a North Carolinian pocketed about the same amount. The report showed that large corporations held 1,045 tobacco farms, but it did not break the statistics into the type of tobacco grown on the farms. Anxious to reap the federal money, several life insurance company representatives inquired of the AAA if their papers were in order.[20]

In the three southern rice-growing states, Arkansas had four contracts in the $10,000 and above category that yielded a total of $69,000, Louisiana had twenty-five that received $484,000, and Texas had eighteen that pocketed $412,000. Altogether, rice growers in the large categories received $9.4 million for cooperating with the 1935 program. Looked at another way, large cotton planters took almost 2 percent of all AAA money in the program while tobacco farmers took but 0.74 percent. Obviously, rice farmers were much larger operators, for they took over 16 percent of the large farm government payments.[21] A thorough analysis of the division of AAA payments would be a significant contribution to the economic history of the New Deal.

IV

Of all the elements of transformation, mechanization proves the most elusive to chart. In a sense, it was like a wave that had gained momentum since the turn of the century. Rice farmers, of course, were highly mechanized, and only during World War II would they turn to combines and reach another stage. Tobacco farmers plodded along with their labor-intensive work cycle until the 1960s, and only in the last dozen years have they turned to harvesting machines.

Mechanization in the cotton belt started in Oklahoma, Texas, and the Mississippi River Delta and spread east, from the area less encumbered with the boll weevil and the legacy of plantation agriculture and sharecropping. Increasingly, farmers bought tractors to replace aging mules, and both tractors and mules coexisted simultaneously. Many commercial farmers took the first step toward mechanization in the 1930s, and they often used government money to purchase tractors. With an assured parity price, they could invest with some certainty of paying off their debts.[22]

According to one study, each tractor displaced several families, and the 111,399 tractors introduced into cotton-growing states in the 1930s displaced from 100,000 to 500,000 families, or from a half-million to two million people. Of the 148,096 fewer farm operators over the 1930s decade, mechanization displaced from one-fifth to two-fifths, and AAA acreage reduction accounted for much of the remainder.[23]

The combination of New Deal acreage reduction and increasing mechanization during the 1930s started a significant shift in southern farm organization. Two studies, one of Georgia and the other of several Arkansas counties, show how traditional tenure

arrangements shifted due to the introduction of tractors. "With
the rapid increase during the past few years of the use of mechanical equipment on Georgia farms," the report began, "com-
plications have developed in the customary rental arrangements
between landlords and tenants." The study concentrated solely
upon the changing relationship between landlord and sharecropper, obviously the most significant sphere of tenure adjustment.
As the report observed, the percentage of croppers dropped 39.6
percent in the decade of the 1930s, and mechanization pushed off
more sharecroppers than had the earlier acreage reduction
policies of the AAA.

The report began with the example of a farmer in the Georgia
Black Belt who customarily ran ten tenant families and twelve
mules. "He bought a tractor and tractor equipment for cultivating, displaced all 10 cropper families and sold 8 of his mules." He
kept two mules to use in small fields, kept two of the families on
as wage hands, and did all the tractor work himself. In other
cases, landlords continued using sharecroppers for cash crops but
utilized tractors to till "conservation crops" and hay for livestock.
Most owners charged sharecroppers for tractor work such as
breaking land and running rows. The cost varied; some landlords
charged for the labor of the tractor driver, others for driver costs,
fuel, and depreciation, and a few simply charged a flat fee per
acre. The families retained either as croppers or wage hands
were the more able farmers.

Other cases from throughout the state illustrated changes in
tenure. One landlord furnished the tractor, equipment, fuel, and
half the seed and fertilizer and divided the crop equally with a
sharecropper. The landlord had formerly used three cropper
families and farmed with mules. The tractor plan had been working for three years, and the report concluded that both landlord
and sharecropper "are well pleased with the change." Most examples showed a basic pattern as landlords displaced tenants,
bought tractors, and increased the acreage tilled by the remaining croppers. In some instances, the cropper's status had been

What of the fate of dispossessed sharecroppers?

eroded with wage work. On one farm, the cropper worked
eighty-five acres as a cropper and sixty-five acres for wages. On
another, "The cropper is cultivating 160 acres of cropland with
the tractor which was previously worked with 5 mules and 5 wage
families." In another case, the owner supplied the tractor and
also allowed the cropper to do custom work in the community
and paid him wages for the work.

In Georgia, the shift from mules to tractors did not require a
large amount of capital. The study focused on a Newton County
farm to illustrate the point. The landlord displaced two of his
three cropper families, sold three of his four mules for $600, and
part of his mule-drawn implements for $100. He purchased a
tractor for $630, and equipment including a "disc plow, section
harrow, planter, distributor, and cultivator for $387." After sell-
ing off the mules and equipment, it cost the owner $317 to make
the shift. He continued to plant the same number of acres but
used one cropper and a tractor. The report neither questioned
mechanization nor speculated on the fate of dispossessed sharecroppers.[24]

A 1938 study conducted jointly by the USDA and the Arkansas
agricultural experiment station weighed the impact of tractors on
plantations in the Arkansas, Red, and Mississippi river bottoms
in Jefferson, Miller, and Phillips counties. Using interviews with
planters, sharecroppers, and wage hands plus AAA data, the report covered 89 plantation operators and 423 sharecroppers and
wage hands. Unlike the Georgia study that included small units
and the entire state, the Arkansas study measured plantations
that averaged over one thousand acres with over two-thirds of the
land in cultivation, mostly in cotton. It pointed out several new
trends in farm organization traceable to government programs
and mechanization. Tenant displacement took place in two periods, it stressed, "from 1933 to 1934, when cotton acreage declined for the second successive year; and from 1935 to 1937,
when there was a marked increase in the number of tractors used
on the plantations."

Not only did some croppers leave farming but also landlords changed the tenure pattern, assigning remaining croppers "nominal cotton acreages" and paid them extra for wage work. Data from two additional Mississippi River counties, Chicot and Mississippi, being studied separately, paralleled that from the other three. These two counties had a 12 percent displacement of resident families from 1932 to 1938. Both counties were shifting from sharecroppers to wage labor. "The number of tractors employed on the plantations in these two counties," the report added, "has increased at a more rapid rate than the number used on the plantations in Jefferson, Miller, and Phillips Counties."

Yet the change to tractors progressed unevenly in the rich Arkansas cotton lands. In 1937 only fifty-six of eighty-nine plantations used tractors, and thirty-six of these had been using them since 1932. Only three had used tractors before 1926. Most landowners used tractors for breaking land and seedbed preparation, and they increasingly used them for hay crops. On traditional mule plantations, the number of "resident families" remained stable, but on tractor plantations they decreased by 9 percent from 1931 to 1937. Families remaining on mechanized plantations became wage hands or sharecropped reduced acreage. The report stressed that the "economic displacement" due to changes in tenure status was "equally as important as the physical displacement of families previously noted." Further displacement, the report noted, had been "held in check by the inability, thus far, of plantation operators to mechanize the operations of cotton chopping and picking." Most planters kept resident families and hired seasonal labor for these chores, but the report predicted that the successful development of a cotton picker "will pave the way for further displacement of resident families."[25]

Paul S. Taylor, who toured the country with his wife, photographer Dorothea Lange, observed the changes taking place in the southern cotton culture. Taylor, who taught at the University of California, specialized in rural labor problems, and he testified before Congress and before the Temporary National Economic Committee that studied the concentration of economic power in

The dispossessed ended up on relief rolls.

the country. Before a special Senate committee studying unemployment and relief, he observed in 1938 that former cotton sharecroppers and wage hands increasingly ended up on relief rolls. Many had been displaced by tractors. "A planter in the Mississippi Delta, to cite an outstanding example," he testified, "purchased 22 tractors and 13 four-row cultivators, let go 130 out of his 160 cropper families, and retained only 30 for day labor." Senator James F. Byrnes, skeptical at this example, asked for the name of the planter, and Taylor replied that it was J. H. Aldridge who farmed near Greenville, Mississippi. Dorothea Lange had taken a photograph of one of the tractors at work in a field. Most of the displacement, Taylor noted, came in the flat and relatively boll weevil-free states of Texas, Oklahoma, and the Mississippi and Arkansas deltas where farmers could easily utilize machinery and profit from a lower cost of production.[26]

Displaced workers, Taylor observed, "are forced into the towns in large numbers and drawn back onto the farms only for short seasonal employment at chopping and picking time." In June 1937 he had watched trucks roll into Memphis and take from one thousand to fifteen hundred laborers to chop cotton in the nearby Delta area. Most, he observed were former sharecroppers. "The burden grows of relief of unemployed farm laborers congregated in the towns and cities of the South."[27] Increasingly, it became obvious that the combination of acreage reduction and mechanization was changing the face of southern agriculture. Partial mechanization with tractors began a structural shift that would be consummated with the perfection of the cotton picking machine. By World War II the last major piece of the mechanization puzzle, the mechanical cotton picker, was ready to be put in place.

Memphis labores to the Delta to chop cotton.

V

The irony of federal intrusion lay not in the fact that the government entered agriculture or that in the 1930s it took control of much of its planning, but rather that it created conflicting programs that largely ignored not only its own role and that of poor farmers but also that of technology.[28] The painstaking studies of tenure, of moving people to more fertile land, and aiding a small percentage of marginal farmers largely ignored the emerging structure of the cotton culture. The scientific arm of the USDA worked to create a new mode of technological production while its social agencies sifted through plans to prop up the old structure. While such contradictions touched the rice and tobacco cultures more lightly, from the 1930s to the 1950s the cotton South metamorphosed from a labor-intensive culture to one that used machines and chemicals, and the production of cotton moved ever westward.[29]

The impact of New Deal policies in the rural South proved complex, contradictory, and revolutionary. The AAA and federal rural programs often aided landowners more than tenants, traditional lending agencies more than borrowers. After years of promotion by implement companies and boostering by the Extension Service, by the mid-1930s southern farmers turned to machines. Despite the surplus laborers clogging the byways of the region, landlords invested their government money in machines and looked with satisfaction at the stable prices produced by government programs. The rural cycle attuned to nature became warped. Tractors prepared seed beds, planted, and plowed the cotton land, while wage hands poured in to chop out weeds and then pick the lint. The human contribution in crop production became fragmented. Many southerners, black and white, hesitantly left the countryside, paused in towns and cities nearby, and moved on out of the South never to return. They took little in the way of earthly goods, but they transferred a rich cultural heritage.

The forces that had begun at the turn of the century at last triumphed, and the South experienced its own enclosure movement. Neither those who left nor their neighbors who stayed behind shared the traditional relations with landlords that had typified southern rural life since the Reconstruction Era. The custom of landlords supplying housing, food, wood, pasture, and hunting and fishing rights receded into memory, and the twenty-seven government agencies, in part, took up the slack as paternalistic provider. In the 1940s, rural exiles found work in defense industries or in the army, and thus World War II, not the New Deal, rescued many victims of government programs and mechanization. The war gave them a job, a purpose. It also became a great divide. After fifteen years of depression and war, the vitality and spiritual reserves of rural southerners and their exiled kin and neighbors were low. They had believed that Roosevelt and the New Deal would bring the millennium, but instead many were ushered off the land and dispossessed of their work and communities. It would be another generation before these Americans and their descendants could look with nostalgia to the 1930s.

The New Deal and Southern Labor

J. WAYNE FLYNT

Come all you poor workers,
Good news to You I'll tell,
How the good old union
Has come in here to dwell

Which side are you on?
Which side are you on?

If you go to Harlan County,
There is no neutral there,
You'll either be a union man
or a thug for J. H. Blair.

It is not surprising in a world of Calvinist religion, Appalachian fatalism, and Manichean simplicity to find so clear a division between the forces of light and darkness. And more objective historians and economists can understand why the author of that song viewed Harlan County without much comprehension of the complexities of the international depression, the economics of coal management, or cash flow problems. Florence Reece was thirty years old when she penned the words, mother of eight children, and wife to Sam, a union organizer who began mining coal when he was eleven. Her father had been killed in the mines while loading a ton-and-a-half of coal for thirty cents: "That's what he got killed for, for nothing. I never knew if Sam would come back when he went to the mines in the morning."[1]

It is tempting to tell this story in terms of the Florence Reeces, the people who lived it rather than the unions they created or the organizers who came to work in their hollows, mill towns, and cities. It is a measure of their economic desperation that tens of thousands of poor white workers modified their individualism sufficiently in the 1930s to join biracial labor unions and bargain collectively. Although they were less than ideal union members, often spurning union discipline in order to launch wildcat strikes or vote for racist politicians who despised unionism, they still constructed the first truly powerful and enduring union movement in the South. Together with their black fraternal brothers, who made much more loyal and disciplined unionists, they helped forge a different kind of region. Despite some statistical qualifications, the New Deal probably had more impact on southern labor than it did in any other region of America precisely because it confronted such enormous barriers of history and society.

I will defend this thesis in three parts: first, the structural changes wrought by the 1930s; next, the broad-ranging interpretive debate over the impact of the New Deal on labor; and finally, the lasting influence of industrial unionism on southern society.

American workers had labored for a century-and-a-half not only against frequent injustice in the work place but against the very structure of American law. During various periods they had been denied the right to organize collectively, to strike, to picket, and to boycott. No sooner did they engage in cooperative action than corporation attorneys dashed to local or federal courts for injunctions. Their leaders were jailed and their unions broken. Labor justly could claim in the 1930s that a sympathetic federal government was a startlingly new experience. To use a baseball term, *they were due*.

The legislative structure put in place during the 1930s can easily sidetrack this story into a fascinating but subsidiary debate. The central thrust of the Roosevelt administration was amelioration of the terrible suffering and economic recovery. Reforming the economic system, providing racial justice, establishing a strong and enduring labor movement, were secondary considerations. Roosevelt had no clear vision of an enlarged labor movement integrated into America's corporate structure. As a consequence, he played a vacillating and ambiguous role in the structural reorganization and strengthening of labor. Unionism owed more to its own lobbying, its political shrewdness, and its friends in Congress than to the administration. But the New Deal was not after all one squire from Hyde Park at the top. It was the new people the president brought into government, his allies in Congress elected partly if not largely because of the people's confidence in him. The New Deal in short was a composite of FDR and the new forces he unleashed. At strategic places I will note Roosevelt's dallying, delay, and ambivalence; but it is without purpose to deflect the central argument of this essay as to whether congressional New Dealers or labor New Dealers or administration New Dealers are primarily responsible for the dramatic changes in labor policy during the 1930s. The point is that the structural changes were substantial and the impact lasting.

Although many legislative enactments and internal developments affected labor in the 1930s, four had particularly extensive impact. First in time came Section 7(a) of the National Industrial Recovery Act in June 1933. Under the terms of all industrial codes approved by the federal government (and rewarded with the famous Blue Eagle), employees had "the right to organize and bargain collectively through representatives of their own choosing", and were "free from the interference, restraint, or coercion of employers of labor, or their agents."

Section 7(a) caused temporary rejoicing among workers as the emancipation proclamation of American labor, but the celebration was premature. It did not specify which management tactics were unfair and the wording was vague and ambiguous. So in August 1933, Roosevelt established the National Labor Board to settle disputes by mediation, conciliation or arbitration. But the

NLB had no statutory or enforcement authority and was too closely tied to the Department of Justice. NLB decisions were openly defied and it was largely impotent. Indeed, during its one-year life only four Blue Eagles were removed as a consequence of unfair labor practices.

The National Labor Relations Board, created in June 1934, was a step forward, but its task remained to settle disputes peaceably, not to guarantee rights for organized labor.

The second and more important development came in July 1935, when Congress replaced Section 7(a) with the National Labor Relations Act, or as it was more commonly called, the Wagner Act. New York Senator Robert F. Wagner and his staff drafted the bill specifically to remedy the defects of 7(a). It forbade employers from interfering with employees exercising their rights to collective bargaining, defined and prohibited a list of unfair labor practices, and created a new and more important NLRB which was empowered to seek legal recourse directly in federal courts. Its function was to prevent unfair labor practices hindering collective bargaining, not as earlier to provide mediation and conciliation. Neither the business community, nor the administration favored the bill at first. Corporate America was nearly hysterical, and Roosevelt disliked the bill because it severed the NLRB from the Justice Department. But after fifteen months of silence, Roosevelt finally endorsed Wagner's legislation, which likely would have passed anyway. After the President's endorsement, most southern congressional conservatives swallowed hard, held their noses, and voted for it, although Senators Joseph T. Robinson and Pat Harrison fought hard to weaken it in the Senate.[2] Just as Social Security became the standard American approach to aging, collective bargaining became the standard approach to labor-management relations.

The third structural change came in wage and hour legislation. In 1936 the Walsh-Healy Act established standards for firms receiving government contracts. Two years later the Fair Labor Standard Act set minimum wage and maximum hour standards for all companies engaged in interstate commerce.

The final element in the new labor scene of the 1930s was the split within organized labor. Long torn by philosophical differences, the AF OF L finally lost many of its internationals in 1935. John L. Lewis of the United Mine Workers led a secession which resulted in creation of the Congress of Industrial Organizations. Rather than organizing along craft lines, the CIO concentrated on entire industries. Because it tackled the toughest unorganized corporations in America and was devoted to social, economic, and political change as well as to unionism, the CIO was iconoclastic. The key southern victories among steel and rubber workers were CIO campaigns, as was the post-1935 failure to organize the cotton textile industry. And the United Mine Workers, which was the most significant union in the South, was also the central force in the formation of the CIO.

The stimulus of an aggressive, new union movement, a sympathetic federal government, and a president committed to organized labor as a major element in his 1936 political coalition created an era of unprecedented progress for labor. Contrasting the 1930s to the previous decade provides some notion of the magnitude of this change. Membership in labor unions stood at 2.8 million in January, 1933, half-a-million less than in 1929, and some 2 million less than in 1920. The movement was bankrupt both of resources and ideas. By 1941 organized labor had tripled its membership to 8.4 million. For the first time in American history, a substantial fraction of the nation's nonagricultural workers belonged to a union (23 percent). In some sectors of the economy growth had been spectacular: the share of manufacturing workers belonging to unions increased from 8.8 percent in 1930 to 34.1 in 1940; 21.3 percent of all miners belonged to unions in 1930 compared to 72.3 percent in 1940. Other industries experienced change but not of the same magnitude: 7.5 percent of all textile workers belonged to unions in 1930, and only 14.3 percent in 1940.[3]

If one concentrates on the extent of change rather than the scale of difficulty, the South was the major bastion that withstood labor's juggernaut. Despite rapid gains in the 1930s, only 10.7

But South only @ W. Ⅱ 90

percent of the South's nonagricultural workers belonged to unions in 1940, compared to 21.5 percent in other regions. By 1953 only 17.1 percent of the South's workers were organized compared to 32.6 percent nationwide. At the end of the New Deal the South's unions tended to be clustered in states employing many workers in manufacturing and mining—Kentucky, Alabama, and Tennessee. The predominantly textile states—Georgia and the Carolinas—were the weakest union areas.

More important than region in explaining unionization during the 1930s was metropolitan influence. Organization of a strategic industry concentrated in or near a major city had a ripple effect on other industries and towns. Birmingham furnishes the best example, where early successes among coal miners provided the base for successful efforts to organize steel, cast iron pipe, textile, and rubber workers both there and in nearby Anniston and Gadsden.[4]

Southern barriers to unionization are well known and need little elaboration: individualism, religious fatalism, racial prejudice, community and employer hostility to outsiders and labor unions, abundant unskilled labor, extensive poverty, large numbers of factories located in rural areas and small towns, and the predominance of the cotton textile industry which successfully resisted unionization.

But before examining how these factors hindered unionization regionally, one needs to place labor in a national context. The central interpretive question is why did organized labor grow so rapidly during the 1930s and what this growth reveals about the nature of American unionism. Beyond the obvious explanations of a sympathetic president, a more liberal Congress, and an aggressive new enthusiasm by labor itself, there are at least three ways of viewing labor in the period. First, it was an extension of the existing trade union movement. The creation of the CIO and modifications of the AFL were merely examples of changing trade union strategies to adapt to new economic conditions. Selig Perlman, one spokesman for this view, concedes that the New Deal

opened the mass production industries to unionism and notes
that division within labor modified the principle of exclusive union jurisdiction. But he still maintains that there was more continuity than change in the labor movement of the 1930s.[5]

In a perceptive recent essay, David Brody agrees with Perlman concerning both the continuation of the American trade
union tradition and the forces stimulating labor upheaval (New
Deal politics, the unrest of industrial workers who were unemployed or threatened by the depression, the tactics of corporate
management, and the role of trade unionism). The central unre-
solved issue to Brody is one of focus and chronology. The key
element becomes the depression itself and the way it broke down
the system of labor control within industry. The depression shattered the prevailing assumptions about welfare capitalism and
allowed the CIO to respond successfully to the new rank-and-file
militancy of American workers who came closer to perceiving
themselves as a separate class than ever before. "Industrial unionism" was the perfect response to this consciousness because it
deemphasized internal differences among workers because of
skills, trades, and races and focused on similarities. Yet it was
traditional in that it channelled them into a trade union collective
bargaining mold despite much leftist rhetoric and some communist influence. In the oft-repeated explanation of John L. Lewis
when warned of communist influence within the CIO: when hunting who gets the bird, the dog or the hunter?

Brody raises another important point which is especially applicable to the South, the issue of periodization. Instead of treating
the New Deal and labor as a phenomenon beginning in 1933 and
ending in 1941, as earlier labor historians had done, Brody pro-
poses to carry the story through the war years in a two-phase
development.[6] The first ended in 1937 with the significant victories of industrial unionism over the steel and auto industries
and effective federal protection of labor's right to organize (the
Wagner Act). The second phase ending in 1945 completed the
basic task of organizing the mass production industries and

stabilizing the new unions. This essential second phase relied not so much on New Deal legislation as on the return of prosperity and high employment, and wartime controls which reduced employer resistance and provided a secure setting for collective bargaining.[7] Brody's thesis is particularly applicable to the South where many battles begun under 1930s New Deal legislation were not resolved until the early 1940s.

A second interpretive framework suggests that the labor movement changed fundamentally in the 1930s. It moved from its older traditions of simple unionism toward a broader political concern for social democracy. During the most militant phase of CIO life, 1936–37, emergence of a labor party seemed a possibility. The union's willingness to engage actively in partisan politics, its interest in social and economic reform, its tolerance of communists and other left-wing elements, and its union democracy and responsiveness to rank-and-file seem dramatic evidence of a new kind of unionism. Brody dismisses the notion of CIO iconoclasm by reminding that the CIO endorsed Roosevelt and expelled its communist elements. Furthermore, its structure was patterned generally after the AFL and its ultimate objective was still a collective bargaining contract.

The AFL, which in this drama is usually cast in the role of "heavy" or ignored altogether, responded quickly and vigorously to the CIO's challenge. Some old-line craft unions adopted new industrial union structures and moved vigorously against unorganized companies. The absorption with industrial unionism which one finds in labor histories written by Irving Bernstein and Walter Galenson obscures the role of the AFL. Although the older structures lost 1.1 million members to the CIO in 1936–1937, the AFL's major affiliates recruited more than 760,000 new members during the same period. And between 1937 and 1939 the CIO actually lost members, growing on a sustained basis only during World War II. During the period of 1937 to 1945, the AFL gained four million members to only two million for the CIO. Further, CIO membership was concentrated narrowly in durable goods manufacturing such as autos, steel, tires, etc., (86 percent of its 3.9 million members in 1945) whereas the AFL penetrated all sectors of the economy. This pattern has caused one historian to conclude recently that AFL-CIO competition was less important in union growth than the influence of new political factors such as the Wagner Act and the NLRB. The AFL and CIO both took quick advantage of these New Deal measures which in the long-run made the federal government the chief arbiter of how unions would adapt to economic changes.[8]

The same pattern occurred in the South during the 1930s with growth in older AFL unions far surpassing the more spectacular CIO victories. In 1939 there were some 627,000 union members in the region. Of these 388,700 belonged to AFL affiliates (102,000 were in the building trades; 146,000 in railroad and related unions; 30,200 in other transportation industries; 23,700 in the food and tobacco industry; 21,700 in government employee unions; and 13,000 in the printing trades). The CIO had only 143,600 members and about 80,000 of these were in the UMW not including 100,000 UMW members in West Virginia. In fairness to the CIO, however, its base in the automobile, rubber, textile and petroleum industries (some 25,000 members) provided the structure for significant CIO growth in the South during the War.

The third interpretive view of New Deal labor emerged in the tumultuous years of the 1960s and 70s. Quite unlike the second view, which believed labor shifted substantially to the left, the revisionist historians of the 1960s interpreted the CIO as just another part of labor's conservative tradition.[9] CIO leaders subscribed to the same "corporate ideology" as businessmen and desired to fit labor into the corporate structure of American life. UMW reluctance to help Harlan County miners in the early 1930s or the later CIO purge of left-wing unions such as Mine, Mill, and Smelter Workers both fit this pattern.

David Brody rejects this interpretation noting that it does not adequately explain the actions of men such as John L. Lewis,

Sidney Hillman, or David Dubinsky. Nor did business so interpret it, bitterly resisting industrial unionism in most cases. Although the right to organize was involved in a New Deal recovery package much desired by corporate interests, neither they
nor Roosevelt had contemplated NRA's Section 7(a) as part of the
deal. This measure was tacked onto the recovery program and
conservatives could not dislodge it. And business evasion of 7(a)
led to the Wagner Act which business fought because it reduced
its power to resist unionism.[10]

Once again the southern experience tends to support Brody's
conclusions. The organizing drive launched by labor in the 1930s
and supported by New Deal legislation fundamentally challenged southern society at four points. First, industrial unionism
posed a serious threat to the major unorganized industries which
repeatedly had defeated AFL offensives. Secondly, the CIO challenged the racial shibboleths underlying southern society.
Thirdly, congressional and intellectual allies of the CIO attacked
repeated and historic denials of civil liberties. And finally, labor
in the 1930s broadened its political involvements.

Industrial Unionism in the South

In many ways, the bituminous coal industry furnished the best
test case for the NIRA. All the troubles of American industry
seemed to plague coal: overproduction, international competition, internal conflicts between companies and regions, labor
turmoil, and lack of industry-wide coordination. Labor's attempt
to impose stability during the 1920s had failed miserably. UMW
membership in 1918 had reached 400,000, but John L. Lewis
tried to expand into West Virginia, Kentucky, and Illinois with
disastrous consequences. By 1930 membership had dipped below 100,000. Alabama District 20 had 23,000 members in 1920,
almost none in 1930. Membership in Kentucky had dropped
from 19,000 to 100 and in West Virginia to only 6,000.[11]

The UMW provides excellent pre-and post-New Deal examples of organizing efforts in the South. The union conducted drives in Harlan County in the mid-1920s, in 1929, and again in 1931. In 1924 the UMW closed down after a brief stay; in 1929 it enrolled 12,000 miners before being virtually driven out. Indeed the UMW was so feeble in 1931 that union leadership urged miners to end their organizing strike and provided little financial aid or relief assistance. Lack of national support and growing hunger turned striking miners bitter and violent. The Battle of Evarts in May 1931, a pitched battle with deaths on both sides, was the nadir of unionism in the South. Both the nearly defunct IWW and the communist National Miners Union sought to replace the UMW, but local mine operators and their private armies proved more than a match for them.[12]

Then came the New Deal and NIRA. The first union leader to fully exploit Section 7(a) was John L. Lewis who launched a drive in 1933 to rebuild his own union. By April 1935, the UMW had enrolled 541,000 members, some 95 percent of the anthracite and bituminous coal miners in the U. S. Many of these victories were in the South. Membership in southern West Virginia increased from 7 in June 1933, to 85,764 in June 1935. Membership in Alabama's District 20 during the same period increased from 225 to 18,000.

Successful UMW campaigns demonstrated the complex factors that figured in such victories. At first, attention focused on the NIRA Bituminous Coal Code signed by industry and union representatives in September 1933, which covered some 4,500 companies with 5,500 mines and 400,000 miners. The codes did raise wages by an average of 5 percent, some seventy cents per ton. As an explanation of union success, however, the NIRA is not very convincing. Southern coal operators often ignored the codes, wage, and hour guidelines. Tougher legislation in the form of the Guffy Act, passed in 1935, won UMW backing and the hostility of coal operators but was declared unconstitutional by the Supreme Court. A revised code enacted in June 1937, was delayed by various stratagems until 1940 when wartime activity made it obsolete. Government regulation tended to reduce the number of serious labor disputes and benefit miners with higher wages, shorter hours, and better working conditions, but it also led to higher production costs which cost jobs in the industry.[13]

Furthermore, determined opposition by operators could avoid both the NRA codes and the UMW. The best example is in Alabama where the narrow coal seams of the Warrior and Cahaba fields were expensive to mine and where many companies therefore rejected the uniform hourly wage. William Mitch and William Darlrymple arrived in Birmingham in June 1933, to organize coal miners, and encountered phenomenal organizing success. But despite the NIRA coal codes, many operators refused to recognize the union and discharged UMW members.

The worst offenders were the DeBardeleben Coal Corporation owned by Henry DeBardeleben, and the Alabama Fuel and Iron Company, headed by Charles F. DeBardeleben, Sr. Antiunionism was a long family tradition. In October 1933, miners at De-Bardeleben coal company's Hull Mine near Dora wrote President Roosevelt that the company was denying them the right to organize as guaranteed in Section 7(a). When they joined the UMW, the company vice-president had ordered the superintendent to fire them. The regional commissioner of conciliation from the Labor Department found the company in violation of 7(a), but the miners complained that nothing had been done. Meanwhile they had lost their jobs and were starving.[14] Even more incomprehensible to the angry miners was the fact that the vice-president who had violated the NIRA code, Milton H. Fies, had just been appointed chairman of the Public Work's Program in Alabama.[15]

The DeBardelebens ignored pressure from the Labor Department and increasingly hostile local opinion. They organized company unions in their mines and paid women to circulate petitions among miners saying that they were satisfied with conditions and wanted nothing to do with the UMW.[16] When the *Birmingham Post* editorialized that the DeBardeleben coal corporation "had systematically intimidated its men against joining the United Mine Workers," the company threatened to sue the newspaper.[17]

Alabama miners had to establish the validity of New Deal rights for themselves by a series of strikes in 1933–1934. Violence was common and the National Guard was sent to the Piper mine (Little Cahaba Coal Company) and to the Coleanor mine (Blackton-Cahaba Coal Company) when pickets prevented strikebreakers from entering the mines and disarmed fifteen company guards. This strike spread to seven thousand miners, and union leaders threatened to call out sixteen thousand more unless the coal board supported the check-off of union dues. William Mitch used his New Deal contacts in Washington to persuade the state relief administrator to allow the distribution of food to striking miners which allowed them to ignore a ruling by the regional coal board ordering them back to work. Finally, on March 14, 1934, thirty-eight companies signed an agreement with the UMW representing 90 percent of the operators and 85 percent of the commercial tonnage in District 20. Wages rose from $3.40 per day to $3.60, and companies agreed to withold union dues.[18]

Two notable exceptions to the March agreement were the DeBardelebens. A federal investigator managed to engineer an extensive understanding between them and the UMW in April, one which the owners quickly broke by planting dynamite on a road leading to their coal camps and mounting machine guns at mine entrances.[19] An investigator from the Department of Labor supported union charges that the DeBardelebens coerced their employees not to join the UMW and warned of impending violence. His prophecy was fulfilled in October 1934, when fifteen hundred striking miners engaged company guards in a gun battle in which one man was killed and ten were wounded. Despite all these efforts, the DeBardelebens remained unorganized, the major exception to the UMW's victory in the South.

If the New Deal could be successfully resisted by operators as ruthless and obstinate as the DeBardelebens, how can one explain the speed and thoroughness of UMW success in 1933–34?

Obviously strikes put great pressure on an industry already badly crippled; but another significant ingredient was support by northern coal operators. They were willing to deal with the union in order to stabilize the industry and force southern owners to pay a wage nearer the national average. Although Alabama operators continued to pay the lowest wage in the industry, the southern differential declined dramatically thanks to NIRA codes and UMW contracts.[20]

Even Harlan county operators finally accepted unionization. The UMW negotiated a contract covering 13,500 Harlan miners in August 1938. The most perceptive historian of this episode in labor history has written:

> The New Deal brought industrial order to Harlan county, an increased share of power and liberty to its miners. In Harlan County, as elsewhere, the New Deal produced significant change and reform, not a Roosevelt Revolution.[21]

Victory over the coal industry inspired John L. Lewis to even bolder exertions, and after forming the CIO in 1935–36 he moved quickly to take advantage of the Wagner Act. His first major objective was a formidable one, the steel industry. In June 1936, Lewis began the Steel Worker's Organizing Committee (SWOC) under the direction of two key lieutenants. Philip Murray, UMW vice-president, became chairman of SWOC, and William Mitch, who had served the UMW so well as District 20 president in Birmingham, took charge of the southern region. The choice of Mitch was fortuitous because he had locked horns for three years with the toughest union busters Birmingham had to offer. Myron C. Taylor, chairman of the Board of U.S. Steel, appeared less formidable to the union after tangling with the DeBardelebens.

Given the antilabor stand which U.S. Steel had taken in the past, the CIO geared up for a long, bitter struggle only to discover that the giant steel maker was ready to come to terms. Four factors apparently led to the historic contract signed by Taylor and Lewis in March 1937. For the first time since 1930, U.S. Steel was making substantial profits. The cost of a strike, even if the corporation won, was not worth the damage, especially after the Supreme Court upheld the constitutionality of the NLRB, which frowned on company unions or employee representation plans. The overwhelming reelection of Roosevelt in November 1936, and the determination of the LaFollette Committee to stop antiunion espionage used by some steel companies also figured in Taylor's decision. Finally, if U.S. Steel had to deal with unions, it preferred a single industrial organization to a collection of craft unions.[22] The key point is that TCI, Birmingham's branch of U.S. Steel, was unionized because it was part of a national corporation whose management was outside the South and was more amenable to unionism and aware of the national scene. Some other steel mills in the Birmingham district quickly fell into line, and Noel R. Beddow, former Alabama director of the NRA, became regional director of Birmingham's SWOC office in July 1936. With a staff of fifteen, he tried to organize Little Steel, which ignored U.S. Steel's precedent. Bethlehem, Youngstown, Inland, and Republic successfully resisted until war pressures toppled them in 1941. Beddow did win campaigns in Chattanooga, Nashville, and Anniston, and by 1940 had thirty-three SWOC lodges in the South, half of them in the Birmingham area. Of the ten thousand southern members, fifty-seven hundred were in Alabama.[23]

One mill that successfully resisted Beddow's efforts was Gulf States Steel Company in Gadsden, Alabama. Gulf States, with three thousand employees, was part of a triumvirate that included Dwight Manufacturing Company, with two thousand textile operatives, and Goodyear Tire and Rubber Company, which employed fifteen hundred. Goodyear had located its plant in Gadsden in 1929 because of the large number of poor white farmers who lived in the vicinity. Prospective workers were asked to pledge not to join a union and were reminded, "there's a barefoot boy waiting at the gate for your job."[24] Aided by a community eager to attract industry and keep out unions, these three companies had made Gadsden perhaps the meanest antiunion town in America during the 1930s.

Attempts to organize Gadsden workers occurred in three phases: after adoption of 7(a); after the Wagner Act and the creation of the CIO; and in response to wartime federal pressure.

The impotent Amalgamated Association of Iron, Steel and Tin Workers attempted to organize Gulf Steel in 1933, but the corporation formed a company union, shut down briefly, and fired two hundred union members. During the Great Textile Strike of 1934, the United Textile Workers of America organized a local, but the company obtained an injunction which broke the strike. The NLRB ordered a collective bargaining election in 1936 under terms of the Wagner Act, but the company refused, forcing the NLRB to file suit. Dwight employed a multiple strategy of legal maneuvering to delay the court case and firing selected union leaders. Intimidated operatives deserted the union and the NLRB dropped the case. This ended union activity at Dwight until the 1940s.

But the main drama occurred at the Goodyear plant. Sherman H. Dalrymple, a native southerner and president of the United Rubber Workers, was trying hard to organize the parent company in Akron, Ohio, and attended a Gadsden organizing rally in June 1936. For his efforts, he was physically assaulted and run out of town. Roving bands of company thugs, including a former Auburn football player, beat up labor activists inside the plant, and thirteen union members were "laid off." Others were threatened and decided to change jobs. Despite advance notice to Gadsden police and the Etowah County sheriff's department, several hundred people attacked union leaders on June 25, 1936. This reign of terror effectively destroyed the organizing effort which followed enactment of the Wagner Act.

Noel Beddow sent an organizer back to Gadsden in May 1938, after Republic Steel purchased Gulf States. The company effectively used racial animosity against the integrated SWOC local, but a Supreme Court decision in the fall of 1940 upheld an NLRB ruling against Republic for unfair labor practices. Again the South was the beneficiary of action against a national corporation; Republic acquiesced to SWOC in 1941. By December 1942, the United Steel Workers (as SWOC was then called) enrolled nearly twenty-eight hundred members in the town.[25]

This foothold persuaded the United Rubber Workers to reopen its drive at Goodyear. John D. House, former president of Local Number 2 in Akron, came to Gadsden in January 1941, to lead the drive. His experience demonstrated the company's determination to resist unionization. On February 16, 1941, five men attacked House while he worked in his office and nearly beat him to death. It took eighty-six stitches to close the gashes to his scalp. When he left the hospital, frightened workers shunned him, and a local radio station refused to sell him advertising time. House despaired of local authorities, and urged URW leaders to raise "plenty of racket in Washington and keep it going until something is done."[26]

Despite all his efforts and successful URW campaigns at three other Goodyear plants, including Akron, the Gadsden management had won again. In mid-July 1941, Robert J. Davidson, the CIO representative assigned to the Goodyear effort, concluded sadly that "to continue pouring money into that situation seems to be just like pouring it down a sewer," and reassigned House to a drive to organize a Goodyear plant in Jackson, Michigan.[27]

Wartime pressure, however, succeeded where three URW drives had failed. In 1942, after years of union complaints and NLRB rulings against the Gadsden plant, a federal appeals court upheld a 1940 NLRB judgment ordering reinstatement of many discharged workers and an end to antiunion activities. Paradoxically, the community had resisted unionization during the 1930s believing that to be the best way to attract new industry and jobs; but by 1943 cooperation with the federal government and the CIO was essential to obtain defense contracts. The change in community attitudes coupled with federal pressure on Goodyear brought a representation election in 1943 which the URW easily won. Subsequently, Gadsden became one of the most solidly union towns in the South; in fact many local people attribute the town's economic decline in recent years to the presence of a strong labor movement. The Gadsden episode also demonstrates the importance of continuing the story of labor and the New Deal beyond the familiar date of 1941, when federal decisions in awarding defense contracts exerted much more pressure than adverse NLRB decisions had. Furthermore, the tortuous path through litigation meant that many NLRB judgments in the late 1930s did not obtain the force of federal court decisions until the early 1940s.

Despite CIO victories among auto and oil workers, its other major effort did not end on so happy a note. The textile industry employed more than a million persons in 1937; the cotton goods industry alone employed more people than either automobile or steel. But the industry was extremely complicated, manufacturing many kinds of textiles (cotton, woolen, worsted, rayon, etc.) and dispersed in six thousand firms scattered across twenty-nine states. Half the industry produced cotton goods and 80 percent of its capacity was in the South; 65 percent of the active cotton spindles in 1937 were in the Carolinas, Georgia, and Alabama. The southern mills generally were located in small towns in the southern Piedmont, which greatly complicated organizing drives. The industry was critical to the economies of many states, providing 500 million dollars in revenue during 1935. Cotton textiles represented 60 percent of the value of manufactured goods in South Carolina, 30 percent in Georgia, 23 percent in Alabama, and 21 percent in North Carolina.[28] Taken as a whole, the textile industry was the largest potential union in America, a delicious prospect capable of making even the most cynical organizer salivate just at the prospect.

The South's fifty-year struggle to acquire the cotton textile industry from New England already had captured most of the nation's spindles, but between 1931 and 1940 the region increased its share from 60 percent to 74 percent. A number of

factors accounted for this shift and none of them made the task of
labor organizers any easier: the North-South wage differential,
the proximity of raw materials, extensive agricultural poverty,
cheap labor, state labor policies favorable to management, weak
labor unions, aggressive community support for the mills, and
individualistic southern society.[29]

Typical of the regional contrast in labor conditions was the use
of females who constituted 39 percent of all southern operatives
by 1930. In New England, state restrictions on the number of
hours women could work varied from forty-eight in Massachusetts to fifty-six in Vermont. In the South the most severe
law was in South Carolina which limited hours for females to
fifty-five; at the other end of the spectrum was Alabama which
had no statutory limitation at all.[30]

So. Car. had to most severe women's law (55 hrs. AL: none

Economic woes within the cotton textile industry caused
owners to seek greater efficiency and reduce operating costs. For
workers, these economies meant layoffs and "stretch outs,"
wherein some operatives were expected to do more work for the
same pay thus allowing the mill to lay off others. Historic grievances over low wages and paternalistic control of the mill villages, coupled with economic insecurity, led to a series of bitter
strikes. In April 1930, the Davis Alcock Hosiery Mill in Gadsden,
Alabama, discharged twenty-six women who had enrolled in a
union. The United Textile Workers' organizer reflected his frus-
tration in comments to a Department of Labor conciliator: he
would not organize again if he could not help the discharged
females; he "would not be a party to taking these people into
deep water and then leave them to drown. When they are discharged at one mill they can't get a job at any other which shows
they are black-listed."[31]

Thirty miles south of Gadsden, women in Anniston's Utica
Knitting Mill walked off their jobs in June, 1933, when the company cut their salaries by 30 percent to 40 percent and instituted
the stretch-out. Management told the women if they were
dissatisfied they "could get out and they [management] would fill

their machines." When four hundred operatives at the Net and Twine Mill across town launched a sympathy strike, their manager complained that the police could not "handle the agitators that were leading this strike and in his opinion probably some communists had gotten in with them [local leaders]. . . ."[32] A strike that same summer by more than a thousand mill workers shut down two mills in Newberry, South Carolina, where the issue was again the stretch-out.[33]

The response of the Roosevelt administration was cautious. The president appointed the Cotton Textile Work Assignment Board in December 1934. It contained both employee and employer representatives but its final report generally exonerated industry and recommended against establishing fixed standards regarding the number of machines an operative could tend.[34]

Another early New Deal initiative derived from the NRA textile codes. Like most southern laboring people, textile workers jubilantly greeted Section 7(a). J. P. Holland, secretary-treasurer of the Alabama State Textile Council, recalled: "When we first received word about the Textile Code, the Blue Eagle, and our right to organize, it seemed too good to be true. It was a real New Deal for us." A year later, Hamilton Basso expressed a different opinion: "Southern textile workers feel that they have been betrayed. . . . When the code went into effect there were dances and celebrations. They now feel that those . . . were a little premature." Indeed they were premature. Of some seventeen hundred complaints alleging management violation of wage and hour codes, the Cotton Textiles National Industrial Relations Board conducted only ninety-six investigations and ruled against management only one time.[35]

In the summer of 1934 textile workers took matters into their own hands. The Great Textile Strike began in Alabama in July when nearly twenty-thousand operatives struck for a twelve-dollar per week minimum wage, a thirty-hour week, and union recognition. Although the strike crippled mills in the Birmingham district, unorganized central and south Alabama mills remained open. The Alabama walkout merged into the largest single strike in American history when workers struck the entire industry in September. Of the four hundred thousand textile workers who walked off their jobs, half were in the South. When "flying squads" moved from mill to mill in order to persuade unorganized workers to leave their machines, violence frequently accompanied them. By September 7 ten people had already been killed, provoking the governors of Alabama, Georgia, North and South Carolina to mobilize state militia. The UTWA was clearly losing the strike and gladly accepted Roosevelt's appeal to end the walkout in late September. The 1934 strike demonstrated the inadequacy of 7(a) and of New Deal labor policy in general. It could neither prevent strikes nor compel arbitration, and the UTWA certainly had no respect for the cotton textile codes.[36]

Passage of the Wagner Act in 1935 rekindled labor interest in the industry. In 1937, John L. Lewis reorganized the UTW which had withdrawn from the AFL during the 1935–36 split. Using the pattern which had worked so well in steel, Lewis created a Textile Worker's Organizing Committee under the aggressive direction of Sidney Hillman. The 1937 CIO drive made substantial progress in northern silk, hosiery, and rayon plants but hardly dented the southern textile industry. By the spring of 1939 the CIO union claimed only 27 agreements covering 27,000 southern workers or 7 percent of the region's 350,000 mill hands.

Two factors inhibited progress of the TWOC. First, Francis J. Gorman, president of the UTWA, resented Sidney Hillman's dominance of TWOC and led a rump movement of the UTWA back into the American Federation of Labor. Secondly, TWOC relied too heavily on NLRB representation election procedure, believing that when it won a majority vote and board certification, a contract would follow automatically. But many mill owners simply ignored the NLRB ruling and refused to bargain with the union. Only when compelled by the courts did they accept unionization. Between 1936 and 1939 nineteen southern organizers and union members were killed during strikes. Witherspoon Dodge, a Congregational minister who had left the Presbyterian Church because of his liberal theology, was beaten by thugs in Fitzgerald, Georgia, and stoned by a mob at Gaffney in his native state of South Carolina.[37] Reflecting on his career as a CIO organizer, he wrote bitterly in 1939:

> The South, geographically and physically speaking, is a part of the United States of America. Socially speaking, it is separated considerably from the rest of the country by mountains of pride and rivers of prejudice and valleys of ignorance and swamps of reactionary stupidity and every now and then washed out with floods of lawlessness.[38]

Perhaps this is too harsh a judgment both on the South and the New Deal. The Fair Labor Standards Act, which was introduced by Alabama's prolabor Senator Hugo Black and strongly backed by FDR, established minimum wages and maximum hours for the textile industry. The NLRB acted on nearly thirty-thousand complaints involving six-and-a-half million workers after passage of the Wagner Act, and courts slowly compelled compliance. James H. Hodges, a careful historian of southern textile unionization, concludes that the years 1939–41 brought stability to textile unionism but that the struggle to establish collective bargaining in the industry failed. He blames this failure on the New Deal, whose NRA was tied to the goal of economic recovery and sacrificed 7(a) to that goal. Even the Wagner Act merely provided a legal vehicle for use of basic union power, which did not exist in the textile industry.[39]

But there was no base in steel either, so a more complex explanation of the failure to organize textiles must consider other issues. The fragmented nature of the industry, its location in dozens of small towns which had no strong labor movement, and the internal split of TWOC and UTWA all played a role in labor's defeat. When textile mills were located in or near large cities with strong union movements, as in Birmingham, the outcome was more favorable. Nevertheless, the textile industry, which was the largest employer of southern labor, remained the major failure of southern unionism during the 1930s and 1940s.

Biracial Unionism

If the failure to organize textiles was labor's major defeat, its attempt to organize biracial unions was its most heroic contribution. Although black workers and unions traditionally had shared many of the same goals, conflict and mutual hostility had characterized their relationship. The AFL by guaranteeing its unions local autonomy acquiesced to racial discrimination. The natural exclusiveness of craft unions compounded the problem. The massive migration of blacks to northern cities during and after World War I created antagonism among white workers who viewed blacks as threats to their jobs. Employers exploited racial animosity to break strikes and delay unionization. The AFL's opposition to industrial unionism further alienated blacks, who made up a significant proportion of laborers in durable goods industries. No wonder black leaders at first were skeptical of the CIO's commitment to biracial unionism. But its organizing efforts in the steel and automobile industries convinced black leaders that the union was sincere, and from 1937 on black journalists and civil rights leaders enthusiastically endorsed industrial unionism. [40]

In the South, the CIO encountered the most formidable resistance to its racial stance. Perhaps for that reason New Deal programs emphasized economic recovery and not special status for blacks. Because 66.5 percent of southern black workers labored in agriculture and domestic service, they were not covered by NRA. And even among blacks who were engaged in industries participating in the Blue Eagle, there was much concern in 1933. Many blacks opposed NRA attempts to end wage differentials based on race or region for fear that equal wages would cost their jobs. Some complained that NRA really stood for "Negro Removal Act" or "Negro Rarely Allowed." Higher wages and the need for greater efficiencies did cost the jobs of some marginal workers, but the loss seemed to affect blacks and whites equally. Black workers also received help from an unexpected source, organized labor. Although white unionists often were no less racist than management, they sometimes fought discrimination against blacks because it hurt all workers, white and black. A study of the NRA in Georgia concludes that black workers in large industries prospered under the NRA. They were not fired and their salaries increased to code standards. The black worker might be in worse condition than his white counterpart, but he was in better shape than before NRA. Also, in Georgia, state NRA administrators were fair to blacks in their application and enforcement policies.[41]

Nevertheless, federal files are filled with complaints of job discrimination from black workers. Ten black carpenters protested to Secretary of Labor Frances Perkins that they were not allowed to work on a dormitory being built at the Alabama Polytechnic Institute (Auburn University) for which the Civil Works Administration was furnishing funds. The carpenters were referred to the state CWA administrator for help in resolving the problem. The point is not that racial discrimination disappeared; it did not. But at least there was recourse.[42]

As in other matters, the earliest test of labor's commitment to racial equality was within the UMW. Historically, southern employers had used labor's attempt to organize blacks as a chief argument against unionism, so Lewis had no illusions on this score. The first test came in Alabama where half the state's miners were black and where racial divisions had hampered earlier organizing efforts. Facing the challenge head-on, Lewis insisted on biracial locals, reasoning that failure to involve black miners would almost certainly defeat the union. By 1935, 60 percent of Alabama's twenty-three thousand UMW members were black. The union introduced the "UMW formula" which became the pattern for other labor organizations in the Birmingham district. It provided for a white president, a Negro vice-president, a white secretary-treasurer, and black minor officials. White men conducted negotiations with white owners while blacks gained union experience and leadership skills. Internally, segregation often continued as black workers sat in a different section of the union hall from whites. But even such limited compromises did not go unchallenged, and one white Alabama union leader accused UMW District 20 president William Mitch of practicing "what the communists preach on Negro equality in the ranks of the United Mine Workers and in organized Labor."[43]

The Steel Workers Organizing Committee followed the lead of the UMW. Its black organizers in Birmingham were highly successful. Ebb Cox, a tall, light-skinned Negro, organized in the black churches, bars, and neighborhoods of Fairfield, and was eventually elected the first black member of Alabama's CIO Executive Board. Dobbie Sanders, an early black member of SWOC, remembered that when the steelworkers ran into trouble they would call in North Alabama coal miners: "Them boys would come in here from Walker County with snuff running down their chins, both black and white. And they didn't take no stuff. If it wasn't for the Mine Workers, we never would have got a union."[44]

Progress came more slowly elsewhere. The Mine, Mill and Smelter Workers tried to organize Birmingham's eight thousand ore miners in 1933, but the struggle was a long and violent one. Eighty percent of the miners were black and union leadership was heavily infiltrated by communists. The amazing fact was not the bitter hostility to mine/mill so much as the number of whites who joined despite its large black majority and its left-wing politics.

Without overstating the extent of New Deal or CIO efforts to obtain racial justice, I believe we should not underestimate them either. Earlier efforts at biracial unionism had been halting and temporary. The CIO provided a continuing basis for such activity despite the political risks involved in such a strategy. And in numerous ways, sometimes direct and sometimes subtle, New Deal agencies and administrators encouraged the activity. During the 1930s for instance, the federal government for the first

time became a supporter of workers' education through adult
programs financed by relief funds. Between 1933 and 1943 WPA
workers' education classes enrolled one million people, including
many in the South. Among these programs was Highlander Folk
School where Myles Horton, Don West, Jim Dombrowski, and
others trained a generation of labor leaders. The "students" were
union leaders who brought specific labor problems to the staff
and fellow students. From its beginning Highlander was open to
blacks and worked hard to integrate its workshops. Much of its
funding came from unions, but it also worked with the WPA, NYA
and CCC to finance its programs in labor and later civil rights
education.[45]

Civil Liberties

Both CIO organizational campaigns and racial policies demonstrated that civil liberties commonly recognized in other regions
were not necessarily operable in Dixie. Although Roosevelt acted
cautiously on this front, aware of his precarious political coalition
and the power of southern congressional committee chairmen,
Senator Robert M. LaFollette, Jr., of Wisconsin felt no such
constraints. Armed with Senate investigative powers, he led his
committee to the most remote centers of antiunion violence. His
hearings on Gadsden during March 1937 attracted national attention to the policies of the Goodyear Tire Company even if they
did not change them. The city's embarrassment and the evidence
of company sabotage of the URW were factors both in the successful NLRB case and the union's decision to renew its efforts to
organize the facility.[46] When John House returned to lead the
1941 effort against Goodyear, he documented violations of civil
liberties in a carefully prepared report.[47]

The company withstood this revelation, but it was no doubt a
factor both in mobilizing federal pressure and in ultimate union
victory. The indefatigable LaFollette also launched an investiga-
tion of the infamous DeBardelebens, and discovered that the

north Alabama coal barons had lent three machine guns to the
West Point Manufacturing Company to intimidate a textile workers' organizing drive.[48]

But the most famous activity of the LaFollette Committee
occurred in Harlan County, Kentucky. Violence and intimidation
were so routine in "Bloody Harlan" that oldtimers said that death
from shooting was regarded as "death from natural causes." Two
days after the Supreme Court upheld the Wagner Act, LaFollette began hearings on violations of civil liberties in Harlan
County. The hearings coincided with the dispatch of UMW organizers for yet another attempt to organize the county, and the
timing was not coincidental. LaFollette used the hearings both to
publicize the outrages committed there and to assist Lewis and
the UMW. LaFollette was aided greatly by the demeanor of the
Kentuckians summoned to testify. Two of them, on their first
visit to a city, preferred riding up and down in the Senate
elevators to testifying at the hearings. When they tore themselves away long enough to attend the meetings, some mine
operators wished they had remained in the elevators. One re-
porter advised a colleague:

> Watch closely when the photographers flash . . . their bulbs.
> All over the room there will be men who automatically clutch
> swiftly at their hips, in the manner of men reaching for their
> guns. Then they look around slowly to see if they've been
> noticed.[49]

Among committee revelations was one Harlan mine owner
who conducted a semimonthly second-hand car lottery. He
forced his miners to buy chances by deducting from their wages.
He disposed of eight of his own used cars in this manner at a
profit of two thousand dollars annually. When one senator suggested that he get out of mining and enter the raffle business, he
complained he would not be able to sell chances unless he owned
a coal mine.[50]

Philip Murray, testifying for the UMW, demanded that the
federal government ensure the civil liberties of union organizers

in Harlan County, but LaFollette concluded that the federal government could do little to help. In this regard he underestimated the importance of the attention which his hearings focused on local communities. Even before the hearings ended, the legal counsel for the Pioneer Coal Company in Pineville, Kentucky, admitted to an investigator that the committee's presence in Pineville had caused his company to sign a contract with the UMW. A week after the hearings concluded, miners held two mass meetings in Harlan County without incident.

For those not so willing to coexist with the union, federal authority proved more determined than LaFollette's estimate. In 1937, the Department of Justice ordered FBI agents into Harlan to investigate charges that coal operators had violated the Wagner Act by conspiracy to thwart union organizers. That September, a federal grand jury indicted twenty-four mine officials, twenty-three lawmen, and twenty-two corporations. The Justice Department for the first time recognized the right of workers to organize as a civil liberty that the government would sue to protect.[51] It was a sobering warning to businessmen and politicians throughout the South.

Southern Politics

Although federal intervention was useful as a final appeal, it was slow and cumbersome. A more immediate goal of labor was to change the local and state political structure. The AFL was a poor vehicle for such action. Historically reluctant to become involved in partisan politics, it was largely impotent in poorly organized southern states. That changed dramatically with the advent of the CIO. Unlike its cautious predecessor, the CIO considered social reform to be germane to organized labor and increasingly turned to politics as the method of such change. This challenge tended to carry the AFL in its wake, making even the older, more conservative organization increasingly active. Even in their respective political preferences, however, they demonstrated differing philosophies.

In the mid-1930s the AFL became more active in southern political campaigns but generally opted for an accomodationist strategy. In 1934 Eli Futch, a veteran AFL campaigner, was dispatched from Washington to spearhead U.S. Senator Park Trammell's reelection bid in Florida. Trammell was a rather ineffective but loyal New Dealer, whose opponent, Claude Pepper, was a liberal young politician who had attracted many defectors from labor's ranks. The railroad craft unions performed particularly well on Trammell's behalf, and their shrewd, well financed effort carried Trammell to a narrow four thousand-vote victory.[52]

That same year the choice in the governor's race in Alabama was more clearcut. William Mitch of the UMW and the Alabama State Federation of Labor worked hard to elect Bibb Graves, praising his "past record of friendliness to the common masses of the people of our state. . . ." Once in office Graves was one of the most consistent New Deal southern governors. Labor had constant entree to him and used its influence to revise Alabama's inadequate workmens' compensation law.[53]

In Mississippi, the senatorial choice in 1936 resembled Florida's earlier situation. Two men sought labor backing in the Democratic primary. The incumbent, Pat Harrison, was conservative but had consistently if reluctantly supported New Deal legislation. Harrison's opponent, Governor Martin S. Conner, was an ally of Theodore Bilbo and a representative of the populistic hill counties. He branded Harrison "Roosevelt's rubber stamp" and advocated a more sweeping and immediate recovery program modeled on the late Huey Long's "Share our Wealth" scheme. AFL president William Green endorsed Harrison, and the incumbent carried all but two of Mississippi's counties.[54]

The political choices in Georgia during 1934 were as obvious as in Alabama. The Georgia Federation of Labor opposed Eugene Talmadge who was campaigning to succeed himself as governor.

Talmadge was both antilabor and opposed to the New Deal. He attacked the NRA for giving too much money to people who did not deserve it. During the midst of the campaign, the Great Textile Strike swept Georgia, and 44,480 of the state's 60,000 textile workers walked off their jobs. Georgia mill owners hired Pearl L. Bergoff of New York to furnish eight hundred thugs who traveled to Georgia armed with clubs, tear gas, hand grenades, revolvers, and shotguns. Sixteen textile workers were killed during the ensuing weeks of violence. Immediately after his reelection on September 12, Talmadge mobilized four thousand National Guardsmen and declared martial law. Hundreds of strikers were arrested and held in an internment camp at Fort McPherson in Atlanta. His actions helped break the union despite his pledges of sympathy for labor during the campaign.[55]

New Deal officials and agencies played no small role in political races despite their official neutrality. In most cases a key issue was the capacity of the candidates to attract federal funds, and that meant a sympathetic reception in Washington. At the state level political considerations often involved labor policy, as in the case of William Mitch's pressure on the state relief agency to provide striking miners with funds. Noel R. Beddow, an Alabama relief official and later regional director of the Steel Workers' Organizing Committee, wrote Donald R. Richberg, chairman of the Industrial Relations Board of NIRA, that state NRA personnel "are keeping in as close touch as is permissable . . . with labor conditions. Especially is this true in the Textile Industry."[56]

Liberal Democratic losses in the 1942 elections, enactment of the Smith-Connally Act in 1943, and anxiety concerning the 1944 presidential election, persuaded the CIO to establish its Political Action Committee on July 7, 1943. Sidney Hillman was named chairman and raised a 700,000-dollar war chest. George S. Mitchell was appointed the first southern regional PAC director responsible for an eleven-state region. Conservative southerners launched a furious attack on PAC-CIO accusing the organization of race mixing and communism. Its close association with the Southern Conference on Human Welfare, a controversial coalition of liberals of both races and sometimes leftist political persuasions, did not make Mitchell's job any easier.

But the results were impressive. Among the successful candidates in 1944 who won with PAC-CIO backing were Claude Pepper (Florida, U.S. Senate), Lister Hill (Alabama, U.S. Senate), Olin Johnson (South Carolina, U.S. Senate), and Albert Raines (Alabama, U.S. Representative).[57] In Texas W. Lee O'Daniel had won the governorship in 1938 despite labor opposition, and parlayed sponsorship of antilabor legislation into a U.S. Senate seat in 1941. The advent of PAC changed the balance of power somewhat, and labor aided FDR's victory in Texas. More significantly, a massive PAC voter registration drive in southeast Texas persuaded Congressman Martin Dies to retire. Dies had chaired the labor-baiting House UnAmerican Activities Committee and had accused the CIO of being dominated by Communists.[58]

Unfortunately, most PAC endorsements and funding had to be provided surreptitiously lest it be a kiss of death. In the early years of PAC only James E. Folsom, running for governor of Alabama in 1946, publicly sought CIO support. The race issue became increasingly crippling after 1944 as antilabor politicians used the charge of race mixing against any candidate endorsed by PAC. But the list of PAC/COPE victories is testimony both to the political sagacity of the CIO and the enduring bifactionalism it helped create: John Sparkman (Alabama, U.S. Senate, 1946, 1954, 1962); Gordon Browning, Frank Clement and Ray Blanton (Tennessee governors, 1948, 1952, 1954, and 1974); Albert Gore and Ross Bass (Tennessee, U.S. Senate, 1952, 1958, 1964, 1964); William Fulbright (Arkansas, U.S. Senate, 1968); Earl Long (Louisiana governor, 1955); Russell Long (Louisiana, U.S. Senate, 1948); Ralph Yarborough (Texas, U.S. Senate, 1957); Terry Sanford (North Carolina, governor, 1960); Cliff Finch (Mississippi, governor, 1975).[59]

As for the attitudes of the South's working masses toward

Franklin Roosevelt, adulation would not be too strong a word. The best evidence came in the fall of 1940. Just before election day John L. Lewis delivered a major political address over three hundred radio stations denouncing the president as a warmonger. If FDR won, he promised to retire as president of the CIO. Faced with the choice of Lewis or Roosevelt, the CIO rank-and-file overwhelmingly selected Roosevelt. Sherman Dalrymple, president of the URW and veteran of the tough organizing campaign in Gadsden, advised the president that labor backed him completely. Though not quite accurate, it was close enough. Even a UMW local in Milburn, West Virginia, denounced Lewis's endorsement of Republican Wendell L. Wilkie as a "betrayal of labor." Lewis could not persuade even his own United Mine Workers to desert the president.[60] To many of them, Roosevelt was the man who had saved their jobs and guaranteed them the right to organize. In a real sense they were wrong; Lewis deserved more credit for expanding New Deal labor legislation by his vigorous organizing campaigns, and Roosevelt endorsed such legislation slowly and sometimes reluctantly. But endorse it he did, and though labor owed more thanks to Robert Wagner and Robert LaFollette than to FDR, it still had a firm ally in the White House. By making the urban working class the cornerstone of the New Deal-Democratic coalition, Roosevelt opted for an historic change in the pattern of labor-management relations in America.

The New Deal left a permanent impression on southern labor. The most essential change was that workers turned to the federal government to redress their grievances. New Dealers in Congress and the White House responded with two profound alterations of the nation's laws: comprehensive and permanent regulation of labor practices by the federal government and a fundamental shift of public policy from neutrality to active affirmation of the right of collective bargaining.

Active government intervention and participation in formulating labor policy had a multitude of consequences in the South:

(1) it reduced wage differentials between workers based on skill, race, and region; (2) it increased the political involvement of the labor movement; (3) it spurred growth in union membership both in the controversial CIO and in the more conservative AFL; (4) it gradually ended belligerent anti-union practices, especially during the 1940s; (5) it diminished the need for strikes over union recognition; (6) it strengthened industrial democracy and civil liberties; (7) it speeded a limited but important change in race relations; (8) it strengthened political liberalism.

Obviously, too much can be made of all this, and I emphasize once again all my initial caveats and qualifications. Organized labor was still weaker in the South than in any other region; it was still vulnerable to conservative attacks for its integrated racial policy; many of its white rank-and-file were as racist as any Americans; and occasionally violations of civil liberties and even anti-union violence continued to occur. But every essay must have a thesis and a conclusion. And I will end where I began, with Harlan County balladeer, Florence Reece. She was right. The "good old union" had come South to dwell.

Labor in the South
(1) still weaker than elsewhere
(2) vulnerable to conservative attacks for its interracial policy

The New Deal
and Southern Politics

ALAN BRINKLEY

In 1949—four years after the death of Franklin Roosevelt, more than a decade after the effective end of the New Deal—V. O. Key, Jr. published an assessment of the state of southern politics that has remained largely unchallenged ever since. He wrote:

> When all the exceptions are considered, when all the justifications are made, and when all the invidious comparisons are drawn, those of the South and those who love the South are left with the cold, hard fact that the South as a whole has developed no system or practice of political organization and leadership adequate to cope with its problems.

The problem was not a new one, of course. The political structure of most southern states, Key argued, was in all essential respects the same structure the South had erected for itself at the end of Reconstruction. Politics in most of the South was oligarchic, reactionary, and myopic. It thrived on rigid control of the franchise by conservative political elites, on a fervent commitment to white supremacy, on deep suspicion of "outside interference" in its affairs, and on a one-party system that had faced no real challenge since the 1870s. The Southern political system had, in short, prevented the development of effective, class-based interest groups that might have threatened the jarring inequalities in the region's social and economic structure. "The South may not be the nation's number one political problem . . .," Key observed, "but politics is the South's number one problem."[1]

97

What was striking to Key in 1949, and what remains striking today about southern politics in his time, is how impervious the system appears to have been to a series of extraordinary crises and changes in American life. The South in the 1940s had recently emerged from more than a decade of economic distress that had affected it perhaps more severely than any other region. And it had emerged as well from a period of national political reform whose major outlines it had supported, in electoral terms at least, more enthusiastically than had any other area of the nation. And yet neither the depression nor the New Deal appeared to have wrought any significant changes in the region's internal political organization or in the nature of its political leadership. In other areas of the nation, the 1930s had produced powerful new political coalitions capable of challenging and at times toppling old structures of authority. In the South, the Depression years had produced little more than what Key described as "weak forays against the established order," forays the established order had generally countered with ease.[2]

The most compelling question about southern politics in the age of the New Deal, then, is why so little seemed to change. Why did the South prove so resistant to the kinds of political transformations the New Deal was helping to inspire elsewhere?

I

Part of the answer, the largest part according to some historians who have examined the South in the 1930s, lies in the nature of the New Deal itself, in its failure or inability to mount any serious challenge to the structure of southern politics. Franklin Roosevelt did, it is true, launch occasional assaults against the conservative political establishment of the South. He did at times attempt to encourage the growth of liberal factions in the region, to promote "forces of change" that might challenge the status quo. But such efforts were infrequent and usually halfhearted. Far more typical of the New Deal were efforts to work closely

not its original intent.

with existing political elites, attempts that not only failed to challenge the prevailing power structure, but often reinforced it.

That Roosevelt did so should not be surprising. The New Deal has in retrospect come to represent a modern, welfare-state liberalism committed to a major expansion of federal power through the creation of a great national bureaucracy; it has become a symbol of the shift of authority away from the states and localities and toward Washington. But if that was the New Deal's ultimate effect, it was not its original intent. On the contrary, Franklin Roosevelt and most of those around him were deeply uneasy about the prospect of highly centralized federal authority and bureaucratic expansion; and they sought constantly to limit both, even as they embarked on the new government initiatives they considered necessary in the face of the economic emergency. They were careful, therefore, to place control of virtually all New Deal programs as much in the hands of local officials and institutions as in Washington. Hence, the tendency of those programs was often less to challenge than to perpetuate existing structures of local power.

a lot in local hands

New Deal agricultural programs, for example, almost always scrupulously avoided antagonizing local farm leaders, even when those leaders were—as was often the case in many parts of the South—powerful, conservative oligarchs, exercising a rigid and oppressive control over the local economy. The Agricultural Adjustment Administration did have in each state a committee of administrators appointed by Washington. Far more powerful, however, were county-level committees whose members were chosen by local farmers and whose leadership often rested in the hands of established local elites. Chapters of the Farm Bureau Federation, which represented the interests of established commercial farmers and paid scant attention to the needs of the far larger number of marginal, subsistence farmers, played a major role in selecting many county agents.[3]

farm policy; rigid control over local economy

New Deal relief agencies, similarly, relied heavily on local officials to administer their programs. In northern cities, that

Relief - local officials, too.

often meant placing control of work relief programs in the hands of established Democratic bosses, a fact that has caused a growing number of historians in recent years to cast doubt on the so-called "Last Hurrah" thesis—the thesis that the New Deal shattered the power of urban machines.[4] In rural areas of the South, similarly, relief administrators, like AAA county agents, were often established Democratic leaders and were perfectly willing to bend New Deal programs to serve their own conservative interests. Southern relief administrators at times discharged employees from FERA, or, later, WPA projects when local landholders needed cheap labor for picking cotton or for other agricultural chores—even though the farm wages were often significantly lower than the relief benefits. Some administrators even complained to Washington that the benefits of their own programs were too high, that they threatened the wage scale of local employers. Such complaints came even though the administration had already agreed to respect the regional wage differentials that kept relief payments in the South lower than those in other regions.[5]

Critics of the New Deal have long maintained that the failure of its programs to challenge the conservative power structure of the South was the result of a failure of will; and it is true that such challenges never seemed to rank very high on the list of New Deal priorities. But even had the administration tried to use its programs to change the political balance in the South, it would have run up against an obstacle far more imposing than insufficient commitment: a lack of bureaucratic capacity. Washington's dependence on local authorities for the administration of its programs was not simply an ideological choice; it was a necessity for a government that lacked any experience of intervention in local economic affairs and that had constructed no institutions to allow it to do so.[6]

At the state level, the Roosevelt administration showed little more interest in challenging the distribution of southern political power than it did at the local level. Rather, as with its treatment of local organizations, the New Deal tended to strengthen, not to challenge, the dominant political factions in state capitals. In part, this was a deliberate, perhaps necessary decision grounded in political self-interest. In many southern states, existing statewide political organizations were so firmly entrenched that challenges to them would have been both costly and unlikely to succeed. And those challenges would likely have alienated powerful members of Congress, whose support Roosevelt believed he needed for his legislative initiatives. If he had ever needed any proof of that, he needed to look no further than his first serious effort to confront a hostile, conservative state organization—his attempt in 1936 and 1937 to strengthen the insurgent liberal faction led by James H. Price in Virginia as an alternative to the powerful Byrd machine. That effort resulted only in strained relations with two important United States Senators (Carter Glass and Harry Byrd), and in no serious reduction in the power of the machine. As soon as the political costs of the challenge became clear to the president, he abandoned Price, restored control of patronage to the Byrd organization, and doomed the insurgents to virtual political extinction. In Virginia, as elsewhere, liberal insurgents found the president an unreliable ally in any battle requiring patience and sustained commitment.[7]

To have expected otherwise from Franklin Roosevelt would have been to misinterpret the president's political instincts in fundamental ways. Roosevelt was a coalition-builder, a compromiser, in purely political terms, at least, a conservative. His goal was not to shatter existing political orders and build his own in their place as Huey Long, for example, had tried to do in Louisiana. His inclination, rather, was to conciliate, to broaden his base of support, to win the loyalties of existing leaders. In the South, that meant not only remaining solicitous of political elites in the distribution of patronage and the administration of programs. It meant avoiding issues altogether when those issues seemed likely to create regional antagonisms. Hence, the New Deal's reluctance to challenge segregation in the South, its willingness to tolerate racial discrimination in the administration of its own relief programs, its acceptance of racial wage differentials, its refusal to endorse antilynching legislation, its notable lack of enthusiasm for supporting union-organizing in the South. Franklin Roosevelt was not interested in provoking a political revolution, and except on rare occasions, he balked at doing anything that would inflame regional sensibilities and jeopardize the stability of his political coalition.

II

Could he have done otherwise? Could the president, had he been so inclined, have used his personal popularity, his patronage, and his funding power to spawn effective "forces of change" in southern politics? Some critics have argued that he could have done so, that in any case there were enough prospects for success that he should have tried.

Among the first to voice this criticism was James MacGregor Burns, in his 1956 biography of Roosevelt, *The Lion and the Fox*. Burns argued that the president could have made use of "vigorous new elements in the Democratic party that put programs before local patronage, that were chiefly concerned with national policies of reform and recovery," progressive elements that might have lifted the party "out of the ruck of local bickering and orient it toward its national program." Had Roosevelt joined hands with them, he "could have challenged anti-New Deal factions and tried to convert neutralists into backers of the New Deal." But faced with this opportunity, Burns observed, Roosevelt declined to take advantage of it and failed to join hands with progressive forces. He was unwilling "to commit himself to the full implications of party leadership" because "he subordinated the party to his own political needs; he thus failed to exploit its full possibilities as a source of liberal thought and action."[8]

It is true, as Burns claimed, that Roosevelt's efforts to reshape the Democratic Party in his own image operated within strict limits. But for the South, at least, there is reason to question the implication that the prospects for the success of such efforts were bright enough to justify the attempt. The pattern of southern politics in the 1930s suggests, on the contrary, that the "forces of change" that Burns and others have touted so enthusiastically were, for the most part, weak and underdeveloped; and that even when strong, they were wedded to visions of change in many ways incompatible with that of the New Deal.

The list of southern progressives who rose to prominence in the 1930s is a familiar and in many respects an impressive one: Governors E. D. Rivers in Georgia, Dave Sholtz in Florida, Olin Johnston and Burnet Maybank in South Carolina; Senators Claude Pepper in Florida and Lister Hill in Alabama; Congressman Lyndon Johnson in Texas, to name only a few. Citing such names, some observers have gone so far as to claim that the South's conservative reputation was really a myth, that the South was actually more progressive than other regions of the country in the 1930s. Others have made the more plausible argument that the list of southern progressives suggests at least the possibility of basic change in the politics of the region.[9]

From another perspective, however, what seems most striking about the roster of southern progressives in the 1930s, aside from its relative brevity, is, first, how fragile the progressives' political bases usually were compared to those of their conservative rivals; and second, how limited was even their commitment to the sorts of liberal reforms that most New Dealers outside the South had come to endorse.

Progressives in the South not as strong as the conservatives.

The fragility of the progressives' political base is perhaps best illustrated by what happened to southern New Dealers after their first flush of success. Rivers, for example, managed election to two successive two-year terms as governor of Georgia; but by the end of the second, the public had already grown weary of his relatively modest reform efforts and of what his opponents charged was his reckless spending. Hence, Georgians were

ready, in 1940, to return the reactionary, anti-Roosevelt Eugene
Talmadge to the state house. Claude Pepper managed to hold on
to his Senate seat through the 1940s, but finally fell victim to
charges that he represented leftist inclinations alien to the South
and lost to the conservative George Smathers in 1950. Lyndon
Johnson, who posed as an ardent New Dealer in his first campaigns for Congress, discovered in the 1940s that his liberal image was a serious political liability in Texas and henceforth rose to
prominence by presenting himself as an archetypal southern conservative. Other progressives who seemed in the 1930s to give
promise of regional leadership—men such as Frank Porter
Graham of North Carolina or Hugo Black of Alabama—tended by
the end of the decade to find themselves more influential outside
the South than within it.

Influential southern liberals were not only relatively few and
relatively weak; they were, in comparison with progressives elsewhere, relatively "unliberal." It would be difficult to find a major
white politician in the South in the 1930s whose position on the
question of race moved very far beyond the region's reactionary
norms. But even using more modest standards of judgment, the
conservatism of most southern liberals seems striking. One of the
shining lights of depression liberalism in the South was the so-
called "Little New Deal" that Dave Sholtz constructed as governor of Florida. And yet what qualified Sholtz for admission to the
liberal pantheon was little more than his willingness to permit
the federal government to spend money in his state. Harry Hopkins and others complained frequently to the White House that
Florida was embracing New Deal relief agencies largely to avoid
having to shoulder any responsibility itself for the indigent; that
Sholtz consistently failed to contribute the state's expected share
to welfare programs. Hopkins refrained from cutting off relief
funding to the uncooperative Florida government only because
he was reluctant to punish the state's unemployed for the failings
of their political leaders.[10]

In South Carolina, two apparently ardent New Dealers—Olin Johnston and Burnet Maybank—won terms as governor during the 1930s and seemed, through much of the decade, not only willing but eager to forge a new relationship with the federal government and the national Democratic Party. Like most other southern New Dealers, however, they were willing to consider such a relationship only within rigidly proscribed boundaries. In 1942, when the Roosevelt administration proposed legislation to make it easier for servicemen to vote in federal elections, both Johnston and Maybank (who was by then a United States Senator) responded with outrage at the possible racial implications of the change and demonstrated a parochial belligerence that belied their earlier enthusiasm for the New Deal. Johnston issued a blunt warning to Washington that "we South Carolinians will use the necessary methods to retain white supremacy and to safeguard the homes and happiness of our people," while Maybank promised that the South would retain control of its own institutions "regardless of what decisions the Supreme Court may make and regardless of what laws Congress may pass."[11]

A particularly vivid expression of the suspicion with which southern liberals regarded their counterparts in the rest of the country appeared in a 1939 article by John Temple Graves II. Graves was a syndicated columnist for the *Birmingham Age-Herald;* he was known for his opposition to racial bigotry and the Ku Klux Klan and for his support for most of Franklin Roosevelt's legislative initiatives; he was, by the standards of most of the South, a leading liberal. But he was also a man with a highly defensive vision of his region's progressivism, a vision that reflected the anxieties of many southern New Dealers. The greatest threat to southern liberalism, Graves warned in a 1939 article in the *Nation,* came not from the region's conservatives, but from "outside liberals," who attempted to enforce a rigid brand of national reform on a region that had its own special needs. On the surface, at least, it was a reasonable position. But

Graves went on to denounce northern liberalism in terms that leave one to wonder whether any meaningful progressive stance could have survived this sort of regional scrutiny.

After expressing his loyalty to Franklin Roosevelt and the New Deal, Graves went on to denounce northern Democrats for their failure, "in their approaches to the South, to separate themselves clearly from a communism which ruling Southerners hate and fear above all else." Organizers of the Southern Conference for Human Welfare, an interracial meeting of liberals in Birmingham in 1938, had, he claimed, done serious damage to the progressive cause in the region by insisting upon defying local segregation laws during their meetings. Liberals throughout the nation who had flocked to the cause of the Scottsboro boys, he argued, had "hurt the case for plain justice among a people who might have been persuaded of the innocence of the defendants but who knew that no matter whose the fault, they were individuals of a low order." According to Graves's standards, in short, northern liberals could expect from the South a commitment to progress and reform only if change did not threaten the political status quo, the racial status quo, or even the economic status quo. (He condemned as well agitation to raise industrial wages and strengthen unions in the South.)[12]

It would be unfair, of course, to conclude that the reluctance of southern liberals to endorse open assaults on the status quo always reflected approval of the status quo. Often it did. But there were also many humane and sensitive southern liberals in the 1930s who believed in racial equality, who opposed the political oligarchies, who wanted change—but who also believed that any attempt to promote fundamental change would have catastrophic results, would unleash terrible bigotry and violence. The cure, in short, promised to be worse than the disease. Whatever the reason, however, whether because of essentially conservative instincts or because of timidity, most southern liberals came to look on the northern brand of New Deal liberalism with deep suspicion.

[handwritten annotation: South liberals looked w/ deep suspicion at Northern... Liberalism]

 ⁴At the heart of this suspicion was not so much opposition to specific New Deal programs or proposals. The southern public, according to public opinion polls, almost invariably favored Roosevelt's legislative initiatives; a majority even backed the president's ill-fated court-packing plan in 1938. What southern liberals and conservatives alike most feared from the New Deal was intrusion, federal interference in the South's right to manage its own affairs and chart its own future. That fear stemmed, in part, from a very real, if defensive, regional pride, which became evident in 1938 upon the release of the administration's *Report on Economic Conditions of the South*. On the surface, nothing would have seemed more likely to inspire the region's liberals. The report described vividly the South's colonial dependency on northern industry, the tragic conditions of its agricultural economy, the devastating effects of its reactionary politics on the region's economic development.

Virtually all southern leaders endorsed some of the report's specific proposals, especially the proposal to eliminate the discriminatory freight rates that northern industry had used for decades to limit southern competition. But the dominant response to the report, from southern liberals and conservatives alike, was angrily defensive. Southerners denounced it as a slur on the entire region, an official reinforcement of old and unattractive stereotypes. When Franklin Roosevelt read the report and announced that he was now convinced that the South was "the nation's No. 1 economic problem," southern liberals reacted not to the implicit promise of federal action to address the problem, but to the suggestion that the North was holding the South up to judgment and finding it wanting. A chorus of protests—claiming that the region was, in fact, "the nation's No. 1 economic opportunity," that the South was really most striking for the dramatic progress it had made since the devastation wrought on it by the Civil War and Reconstruction, that what it really needed was "to be left alone"—all but drowned out whatever positive impact the report might have had.¹³

But regional pride took second place to regional fears in inspir-
ing southern opposition to outside intervention in its affairs. That
was nowhere clearer than in the region's response to Roosevelt's
attempt to influence two United States Senate elections in his
famous and ill-considered "purge" campaign in 1938. The president was, for once, trying openly to use his popularity in the
region to support challenges to two of the South's most reactionary figures: Senator Walter George of Georgia and Senator El-
lison D. ("Cotton Ed") Smith of South Carolina. Both were old
men who had become deeply alienated from the president and
his programs; both were facing primary challenges from younger
politicians who identified themselves openly with the New Deal;
George, at least, was, according to early soundings, politically
vulnerable.[14]

But when Roosevelt traveled first to Georgia and then to South
Carolina and openly appealed to its citizens to unseat the incum-
bents and send to the Senate men of progressive vision, he
evoked reactions so hostile, from across the entire breadth of the
political spectrum, that he demolished whatever chance there
might once have been of unseating either man. The issue, after
the president's visit, became not the records of George and
Smith versus the records of their opponents. It became "outside
interference," the right of the South to determine its own destiny
and choose its own representatives. Walter George, predictably,
decried Roosevelt's intervention in the campaign as a "second
march through Georgia," a new "carpetbag invasion." Smith,
equally predictably, evoked similar images of the Lost Cause
with his defiant statement before a statue of Wade Hampton that
"No man dares to come into South Carolina and try to dictate to
the sons of those men who held high the hands of Lee and
Hampton."[15]

But somewhat less predictable, perhaps—and certainly more
revealing—was that southern liberals reacted with similar hostility and consternation. Even those who might otherwise have
been inclined to support the challenges to George and Smith

retreated in the face of Roosevelt's tactics; acquiescence in this "meddling" in state politics, they believed, was both politically and ideologically untenable. One example was the *Atlanta Constitution*, a major organ of moderation and progressivism in the South, a frequent critic of Walter George's conservative, anti-New Deal stances. After the 1938 primary, the *Constitution* published an editorial assessing the results. It praised Georgia voters for their good sense in reelecting Governor E. D. Rivers over a conservative opponent and defeating Eugene Talmadge's bid for the Senate. But it rejoiced above all in the victory of Senator George. The issue in the race, the paper claimed, "was whether the Democratic voters of a state should decide for themselves who was to speak for them at Washington."[16]

Lurking not far beneath the surface, of course, was a much greater fear, shared by liberals and conservatives alike: that outside intervention in southern politics, in whatever form, would inevitably lead to an assault on the region's racial institutions. Again, the *Atlanta Constitution* drew the connection as explicitly as the most reactionary southern leader. Roosevelt's attempt to purge Walter George, its editorial writers claimed, was part of the president's effort to win passage of "the vicious, dangerous and cruel anti-lynching bill. A bill that would forever make the sovereign states but chattels of the central government."[17]

III

If it had not been evident before, the response to Roosevelt's 1938 campaign made clear that the liberal forces in the South were too feeble, too divided, and too limited in their commitment to reform to provide a promising basis for change. But to say that is only to ask, not to answer, the most important questions about the South's resistance to the New Deal's brand of political change: Why was southern liberalism so weak? Were the conservative regimes so powerful and popular that they were invulnerable to challenge? Were southern voters so unanimous

in their support for the status quo that conflict had disappeared
from the region's politics?

Clearly that was not the case. Southern political life in the
1930s was, in most of the region at least, fraught with conflict. In
almost every state, factional divisions were apparent that at least
vaguely reflected class divisions. Challenges to conservative candidates were constant and not infrequently successful. There was
in southern politics a level of conflict and insurgency that seems
at first to belie the weak and tentative picture of New Deal
challenges to the existing order.

It was, however, an insurgency that had little in common with
the New Deal and that often found itself as much opposed to
national liberalism as to local conservatism. For the most powerful antiestablishment tradition in the South was not progressivism, but populism; and the most successful insurgents in
the 1930s, as in the four decades before, were advocates of a
vision of reform far different from that of the New Deal.

The most conspicuous and most successful southern insurgent,
of course, was Huey Long of Louisiana. Whatever we might
think of Long's methods, he clearly represented the "forces of
change" in the politics of his state; his opponents were largely
what remained of one of the South's most stubborn and reactionary oligarchies. And yet Long's relationship with the New Deal
was troubled from the start; by the end of 1933 he was among
Roosevelts's most vociferous and dangerous foes, and the president had allied himself with the conservative opposition in Louisiana.

In part, the break between Long and Roosevelt was a result of
purely personal and political animosities. Both were ambitious
and aggressive leaders; neither was willing to contemplate standing in the shadow of the other. But the break also reflected a
basic difference in the two visions of reform Long and Roosevelt
had come to represent. To Long, the greatest danger to
America's future—and the greatest drag on its present prosperity—was concentrated wealth and power, the ability of a few

powerful men and institutions to govern the lives of the many. The mission of reformers, therefore, was to oppose centralization of power and restore to individuals and communities control over their own lives. That meant, of course, doing battle against the great financial institutions, against the excessively wealthy, against corporate tyranny. But it also meant resisting the growth of a powerful federal bureaucracy, for an overbearing central government was as capable of oppressing the people as any private power center.

Such concerns put Long squarely at odds with the major thrust of the New Deal. Despite Roosevelt's own reservations about big government, the reforms of the 1930s worked inexorably to create an ever-larger national bureaucracy and to intrude the national government ever deeper into the affairs of individuals and localities, developments against which southern insurgents generally recoiled.[18]

It was not only in Louisiana that they recoiled. Eugene Talmadge in Georgia rose to power, like Long, through strident attacks on the ruling oligarchies; but Talmadge was an equally embittered critic of the "communistic, free-spending" policies of the New Deal. Theodore Bilbo in Mississippi first emerged in state politics as a foe of the Old Guard and won a Senate seat in 1934 as a scourge of the conservative elite; but his subsequent career was characterized by a sour, virulently racist battle against federal incursions into local affairs.[19]

The dominant insurgent force in the depression South, in short, was not the weak and tentative group of southern liberals who identified with the New Deal. It was a force that drew from the region's own populist traditions, one that could produce both radical and reactionary demands, one that could find expression simultaneously in a Huey Long and a Eugene Talmadge. And it was, above all, a force that looked with equal hostility at the conservative aristocrats who dominated Southern politics and the social democratic liberals who were building a powerful and intrusive new federal bureaucracy. Franklin Roosevelt never en-

tirely understood either the strength or the nature of this powerful southern insurgent tradition; but he understood it well
enough to know that it was no friend of his New Deal.

IV

What, then, must we conclude about the impact of Franklin
Roosevelt and the New Deal on the politics of the South? Clearly
the New Deal wrought no internal revolution in southern politics. Few southern states emerged from the depression with
political systems more fluid and progressive than those with
which they had entered it. No equivalent appeared in the South
of the Roosevelt coalition that was reshaping the Democratic
party in the rest of the country. There is, on one level at least,
little reason to question the conclusions of such scholars as V. O.
Key, Jr., George B. Tindall, James T. Patterson, and others that
in political terms the New Deal passed through the South leaving
few discernible changes in its wake.[20]

And yet, little more than twenty years after Franklin
Roosevelt's election to the presidency, fewer than ten years after
his death, a series of profound transformations did begin to occur
in southern social, economic, and political life. This Second Reconstruction, arguably the most significant period of change in
the entire history of the South, was not the direct work of the
New Deal. But it was to a striking degree a result of New Deal
policies that, indirectly and often inadvertently, paved the way
for the transformation to come.

Some of those policies helped to transform the South's own
social and economic structure. New Deal agricultural programs,
for example, unintentionally but decisively worked to push
southern tenant farmers and sharecroppers off the land. In the
short run, the result was enormous hardship for the displaced
farmers. In the long run, however, the result was a radical
change in the structure of the South's agricultural economy and a
decline in the power of the Black Belts, which had dominated the
region's politics since the end of Reconstruction. The exodus of

sharecroppers from the land was responsible, too, for a major increase in the black population of southern cities; and it was from among these urban blacks that the early civil rights movement drew its greatest strength.[21]

But the New Deal was even more effective in laying the groundwork for the Second Reconstruction through its impact outside the South, and above all through its effect on the national Democratic party. Franklin Roosevelt may not have succeeded in wedding southern Democrats to a modern, statist liberalism; but he was highly successful in imposing a new liberal outlook on the party as a whole. More important, Roosevelt was able to turn the national Democratic party into a powerful new majority coalition capable, as it had never been before, of winning elections and dominating government even without support from the South.

For nearly a century, the South's position within the Democratic party had been the region's most effective tool for maintaining its power and autonomy within the larger American society. For the national party to have any hope of victory, it had always had to rely on the solid, one-party South for support. The Democrats could nominate a presidential candidate uncongenial to its southern members only at the party's peril, as it discovered when it selected Al Smith in 1928. The South, in short, held a crucial balance of power in Democratic politics, and because of that it had almost always been able to prevent any federal initiatives that might have threatened its conservative institutions or its hierarchical social structure.[22]

Franklin Roosevelt's creation of a new and vastly more powerful Democratic coalition shattered the South's grip on the party forever. No longer could the region hold Democratic presidential candidates hostage to its conservative demands; Roosevelt would have won all four of his national elections even had he received not a single electoral vote from the eleven ex-Confederate states. No longer could the South exercise a veto over the party's choice of national candidates; the traditional two-thirds rule at national Democratic conventions, whereby Southern delegates could block any presidential prospect not to their liking, was abolished in 1936. No longer could the South be certain of dominating the Democratic congressional caucus; it received bitter evidence of that in 1937, when Senate Democrats passed over Pat Harrison of Mississippi, the overwhelming choice of southerners, and, responding to Presidential pressure, elected Alben Barkley of Kentucky majority leader instead. And no longer could southern Democrats impose their racial views on the party as a whole; the sudden and virtually total shift of northern black voters from the Republican party to the Roosevelt coalition in 1936 meant that the national Democratic leadership could not much longer ignore the legitimate demands of black Americans.[23]

The full implications of such changes were not immediately evident to Franklin Roosevelt. They were not entirely clear to Harry Truman, or even, at first, to John F. Kennedy. But ultimately the national Democratic party did move, prodded by the courts and by rising black protests, to ally itself firmly with the civil rights movement and to launch a frontal assault on the southern political system. It was able to do so in the 1960s at least in part because of the political transformation Franklin Roosevelt had wrought thirty years before.[24]

In a sense, then, the most accurate and presient observers of southern politics in the 1930s were the very men whose bitter opposition to the New Deal made them seem the least enlightened of all political figures: the embittered Old Guard conservatives of the South. For it was they who saw more accurately than anyone else what the political changes of the 1930s would ultimately mean to their region. They were often unhappy, of course, about what the New Deal was doing within the South. But what most alarmed them was what it was doing in the North. They realized that the Democratic party as they had known it was vanishing, and that a new coalition was emerging in which they could never again hope to play a decisive role. They realized that this new coalition, in which blacks, and unions, and committed northern liberals played so important a part, would not for long be content to leave the South and its institutions alone. They realized that the South was becoming more isolated from national politics than ever before, and thus weaker, more vulnerable to assaults from a hostile outside culture. Resistance to change from within would not be enough in the new world the New Deal was shaping. Political forces were gathering in the North that would ultimately impose changes on the South from without.

"The catering of our National Party to the Negro vote is not only extremely distasteful to me," Josiah Bailey wrote in 1938, "but very alarming to me. Southern people know what this means, and you would have to be in Washington only about three weeks to realize what it is meaning to our party in the Northern states." Carter Glass, a year earlier, expressed similar alarm. "To any discerning person," he wrote, "it is perfectly obvious that the so-called Democratic party at the North is now the negro party, advocating actual social equality for the races; but most of our Southern leaders seem to disregard this socialistic threat to the South in their eagerness to retain Mr. Roosevelt in power."[25]

Such statements clearly exaggerated the Democratic party's commitment to racial reform in the 1930s, but they reflected a remarkably accurate vision of what was to come, a vision that haunted southern conservatives such as Carter Glass with an almost violent intensity. Glass suggested as much in a letter to Lewis Douglas in 1935. "Now is about as good a time as anybody could find to die," he wrote, "when the country is being taken to hell as fast as a lot of miseducated fools can get it there. Nevertheless, it would be interesting to live long enough to see the thing tumble." Glass died in 1946, with the South he knew and loved and defended, a South whose politics rested on white supremacy and on rigid hierarchical rule by conservative political elites, still largely intact. But had he lived a few years longer, he would have seen the thing begin to tumble. And as he had predicted, it would tumble finally in large part because of changes that Franklin Roosevelt and his New Deal had set in motion.[26]

The Impact of the New Deal on Black Southerners

HARVARD SITKOFF

We did not dare to breathe a prayer,
 Or to give our anguish scope;
Something was dead in each of us,
 And what was dead was Hope.

OSCAR WILDE
The Ballad of Reading Gaol

The New Deal brought to black southerners both the change of hopefulness and the continuation of suffering and misery. More potent in promise than in performance, the New Deal significantly conditioned the future of Afro-Americans but could not escape the black past. President Franklin Delano Roosevelt, whatever his own racial inclinations or ideology, had no *tabula rasa* upon which to work. The heritage of racism shaped the circumstances in which the New Deal operated. It set the limits on possibilities for racial reform in the 1930s. And because the hand of history weighed more heavily on certain regions, the New Deal positively affected blacks less in the South than in the North, and rural southern blacks least of all.[1]

Past politics severely circumscribed the potential of a new deal for black southerners. Because of an entrenched one-party system in Dixie, Democratic weakness above the Mason-Dixon line in the 1920s, and the continuation of the seniority rule to determine congressional power, Roosevelt had little alternative to seeking the support of, and capitulating to the racism of, the white southerners who controlled Congress. He needed their votes for New Deal legislation and appropriations, and the president would take no action on the racial front that would estrange the white southern politicians who commanded over half the committee chairmanships and a majority of leadership positions in every congressional session during the 1930s. "I did not choose the tools with which I must work," Roosevelt explained when declining to press for antilynching legislation:

> Had I been permitted to choose them I would have selected quite different ones. But I've got to get legislation passed by Congress to save America. The Southerners by reason of the seniority rule in Congress are chairman or occupy strategic places on most of the Senate and House committees. If I come out for the anti-lynching bill now, they will block every bill I ask Congress to pass to keep America from collapsing. I just can't take that risk.

Powerful traditions of decentralization and states' rights also undermined the quest of Afro-Americans for equitable treatment in the Great Depression. The local administration of relief and recovery projects, despite numerous executive orders and legislative clauses prohibiting racial discrimination in the New Deal, left southern blacks at the mercy of those planters, industrialists, union chieftains and political officeholders who stood to profit the most by continuing to oppress Afro-Americans. Those who made the decisions at the local level made sure black southerners never shared fully or fairly in the material benefits of the New Deal.[2]

The deficiencies of broker state leadership for the least influential, moreover, prevented blacks from receiving the kind and amount of governmental assistance they desperately needed. A political system dispensing aid on the basis of the strength of the groups demanding it necessarily worked to the disadvantage of

the largely poor and unorganized black community. As Henry
Lee Moon of the National Association for the Advancement of
Colored People wrote:

> The public interest, democratic principles, justice, ethics, or
> even the law are seldom the bases upon which conflicts are
> resolved. Faced with the necessity of resolving a conflict, ad-
> ministration invariably yields to that group which can bring the
> greatest pressure to bear, illustrating anew that government in
> a democracy is government by compromise. Too frequently
> this compromise is characterized by the forced yielding on the
> part of the weaker to the stronger of two contending
> groups. . . . It is obvious that under such conditions, the claims
> of the Negro, however sound, just and legal, are seldom
> granted when they appear to conflict with the claims of a white
> group.

Southern blacks could not get a new deal when their oppressors
held all the power cards and could stack the deck against Afro-
Americans.

In addition, the very ubiquity of the worst depression in
American history determined the limited parameters of the New
Deal's efforts to remedy the plight of blacks. Hard times defined
Roosevelt's mandate and kept the pressure on the New Deal to
promote economic recovery at the expense of other needed
changes. All else had to wait. "First things come first," the President repeated again and again, "and I can't alienate certain votes
I need for measures that are more important at the moment by
pushing any measures that would entail a fight." Roosevelt would
not permit New Deal solicitude for blacks to jeopardize the economic reconstruction that he and the vast majority of the American people considered their immediate and preeminent priority.
Therefore caution, often timidity, governed the New Deal's fundamental approach to racial matters in the South.[3]

Most importantly, three centuries of southern history prior to
the New Deal had trapped the mass of blacks in what Oscar
Lewis would later call the "culture of Poverty." The wrongs of the
past continued to injure blacks who sought to survive the depres-

sion. Millions of blacks in the 1930s remained enslaved by disease and disfranchisement, by a dearth of opportunity for employment and education, by social disorganization and dormancy, by isolation and intimidation. Fear, weakness, and resignation bred a crippling paralysis of will to struggle. Those most likely to resist oppression went north when they could, convinced that migration was the surest path to advancement. Those that stayed lacked the wherewithall to overcome those insisting that they remain the mudsill. Their debilitated status left black southerners without the weapons to fight for the rights of citizenship or a rightful share of New Deal largess. The heritage of black poverty and powerlessness underlay the constraints on Roosevelt, and the New Deal's failure to attack Jim Crow or to succor southern blacks to the extent warranted by their distress.[4]

The early New Deal efforts at economic recovery starkly revealed the institutional and structural determinants inhibiting salutary change for black southerners. Afro-Americans played no role in the planning or implementation of the programs handled by the National Recovery Administration (NRA), the Agricultural Adjustment Administration (AAA), and the Tennessee Valley Authority (TVA). They had no influence with the officials who managed these matters. And they could hardly gain from policies which callously neglected those at the bottom rungs of the economic ladder.

Quickly following its inception, Afro-Americans jibed that NRA meant "Negro Run Around," "Negro Removal Administration," or "Negroes Ruined Again." The NRA primarily affected black southerners by increasing the prices they had to pay as consumers and by inducing employees to replace black labor with white workers. The NRA's effort to raise labor standards largely bypassed southern blacks since the wage codes excluded those who toiled in agriculture and domestic service. Less than one in four employed blacks worked in industry or commerce. In addition, the manufacturing and retail codes of the NRA were heavily weighted in favor of large-scale, efficient, modernized enter-

prises, and against those firms operating at the margins of the
economy, which included the bulk of southern black businesses.
Consequently, the NRA hastened black bankruptcies and forced
disadvantaged black entrepreneurs to close shop and join the
ranks of the unemployed.

The NRA's requirement that labor receive higher wages,
moreover, led to thousands of black workers being displaced by
white employees. The NRA certainly did not initiate this process.
Given the surplus of available white labor, precious few southern
industrialists saw any reason to hire blacks. But, ironically, the
NRA hastened the mass firing of Afro-Americans by not acquiesc-
ing to the white southern demand for a racial differential, a lower
wage scale for blacks. Few southern bosses could stomach the
notion of nonracist equal pay for equal work; and when the NRA
increased the average wage in tobacco manufacturing from 19¢ to
32¢ an hour, and the Fair Labor Standards Act later raised it to
65¢ an hour, the upshot was a halving of black employment and a
simultaneous gain in the number of white workers by more than
40 percent. For most southern black laborers, the only alternative to displacement was acceptance of spurious occupational
classifications. These meant either lower wages than whites received for the same work, as happened in the southern foundries,
or exclusion from NRA coverage, which transpired for the
thousands of blacks employed in southern cotton oil and textile
mills. Few blacks dissented when the Norfolk *Journal and Guide*
categorized the Blue Eagle as "a predatory bird instead of a
feathered messenger of happiness."[5]

The administration of the Agricultural Adjustment Act proved
even more harmful for southern blacks. The AAA aimed to raise
farm prices by creating scarcity; it provided subsidies for farmers
who restricted acreage and crop production. But, never intend-
ing to reform landlord-tenant relationships, the AAA eschewed
safeguards to protect the exploited landless peasantry that constituted a quarter of the southern population. The result for more
than 5.5 million southern whites and nearly 3 million southern

blacks was either the forced exodus from the lands they toiled or the worsening of a miserably poor existence marked by chronic squalor and servility.

The AAA cotton program did little for southern tenant farmers that a plague of boll weevils could not have done. It reduced cotton acreage, and acquiesced in the massive cheating of crop-pers out of their share of the subsidy and in the eviction of tenants whose labor was no longer needed. This callous indiffer-ence to the plight of the South's "forgotten farmers" by the large landowners who dominated the county committees, abetted by the Farm Bureau—Extension Service—land grant college axis which set agricultural policies in Washington, undoubtedly reflected as much class as racial bias. But because more than three out of every four black farmers worked land they did not own, compared to slightly less than half the white farmers in the South, and because black agricultural operators constituted some 40 percent of all employed black southerners, the tragic harm perpetuated by the AAA wreaked epidemic affliction on Afro-Americans. Instead of higher incomes, the AAA brought greater indigence to the black tenantry.[6]

The economic boom promised by the Tennessee Valley Au-thority proved similarly illusory. The TVA's vaunted rhetoric of "grassroots democracy" once again meant local control by those southern whites most determined to prevent Afro-Americans from getting a new deal. Those who had traditionally oppressed blacks in the Valley stayed "in the saddle," and white racism rode high. White southerners excluded blacks from living in the new model town of Norris; segregated work crews relegated blacks to the least skilled, lowest paying jobs; refused to admit blacks to TVA vocational schools or to training sessions in foremanship; denied blacks clerical positions; established racially separate em-ployment offices and drinking fountains; and Jim-Crowed blacks in housing and recreational facilities. Although TVA's employ-ment situation gradually changed for the better for blacks, so that by the end of the decade the number of blacks in the work force and their percentage of the total payroll constituted a higher proportion than their population in the area, TVA continued to conform to the racist byways of the region. Segregation and white supremacy remained inviolate.[7]

The recovery program simply did not take the needs of black southerners into account. It sought to restore the morale and jobs of middle-class America. It never contemplated reforming the structural bases of black impoverishment and infirmity. NRA administrator Hugh Johnson would not permit his subordinates even to consider the special plight of blacks in the South. TVA chairman Arthur Morgan, ever-fearful of provoking local white hostility to the Authority, would offer Afro-Americans nothing more than the admonition that they continue "inching along." And Cully Cobb, the head of the Cotton Section, implanted into AAA policies all the prejudices acquired from a lifetime of work with the white southern agricultural establishment.[8]

The relief and welfare operations of the New Deal, on the other hand, did assist black southerners to a significant extent. At the least, they enabled Afro-Americans to survive the depression. More sensitively administered, overall, these New Deal programs took some real strides toward ameliorating black distress. In the face of strident southern white opposition, such New Dealers as Will Alexander, Harold Ickes and Aubrey Williams battled for a fair share of relief for blacks. Although their commitment proved salutary, their accomplishments remained limited. Black southerners endured, but did not advance in the 1930s. The New Deal could neither aid Afro-Americans to the extent their privation required nor vanquish Jim Crow in the South.

Robert Fechner never tried. The director of the Civilian Conservation Corps (CCC), a southerner and former head of a white-only labor union, Fechner even sought to impose segregation in northern locales that opposed Jim Crow. Throughout the South, Fechner cooperated with state directors of selection like John de la Perriere of Georgia who desired to see black youth only chopping cotton, and who argued that "there are few negro families

who . . . need an income as great as $25 a month." Despite an
unemployment rate for young black males twice that of white
youth, the southern local officials who picked the CCC enrollees
consistently gave preferences to whites. Blacks constituted less
than 3 percent of the first 250,000 in the CCC. Counties with
black majorities in Georgia had no blacks in the CCC, and Mississippi, over half-black, permitted but 1.7 percent of its CCC allotment to go to Afro-Americans.

Gradually, protests from Negro organizations and pressure
from New Dealers sympathetic to the plight of blacks forced
Fechner to relent, somewhat. Although blacks in the South
stayed in segregated CCC units, were kept out of training programs that would lead to their advancement, were generally excluded from educational and supervisory positions, and continued to remain numerically underrepresented, their numbers
and opportunities slowly increased. By late 1936, they made up
some 6 percent of the youths in the Corps, nearly ten percent a
year later, and 11 percent in 1938. That year about 40,000 young
blacks were sending $700,000 a month home to their parents and
dependents. By the start of 1939, almost 200,000 blacks had
served in the CCC, and, because the defense boom caused a drop
in white enrollments, when the Corps ended in 1942 the number
of blacks who had joined the CCC totaled 350,000. Over 40,000
Afro-Americans who had entered the CCC as illiterates had
learned to read and write.[9]

Despite the perpetuation of Jim Crow, it is obvious how much
such assistance meant to blacks. And a hint of a new deal did
appear in many relief and welfare operations. The Unemployment Relief Act of 1933, setting up the Federal Emergency Relief Administration, specifically banned racial discrimination, and
Harry Hopkins, FDR's choice to head the relief program, consci-
entiously worked toward that goal. Both FERA and the Civil
Works Administration, the work-relief effort of the winter of
1933–34, sought to provide adequate allotments without regard
to race. But resistance from southern whites came swiftly. They

found CWA's uniform wage scale and FERA's equal relief grants bitter pills to swallow. Complaints poured in of blacks spoiled by relief, no longer beholden to local landlords, no longer hungry and a willing source of cheap labor, earning more on work-relief than white laborers in private enterprise.

Relief thus jeopardized dearly held class and racial arrangements, and Hopkins's resolve slackened. New regulations prohibited relief payments from exceeding prevailing salaries in a region, lowered the hourly minimum wages on work-relief, permitted the closing of relief projects during the cotton-picking season to provide the labor planters desired, and gave great discretion to state and local relief officials in the administration of their programs. Consequently, the Negro's chance for obtaining relief, and the amount of relief, was greatest in the urban North, less in the cities of the South, and least of all in the rural South, where the majority of Afro-Americans still lived in the 1930s. Discrimination was rife and blacks remained at the mercy of the lily-white personnel in local relief offices. Yet, federal relief enabled southern blacks to survive the depression. Although they never received assistance commensurate with their need, blacks comprised a higher proportion of the work relief rolls than their percentage of the population almost everywhere in the South throughout most of the decade.[10]

Much the same pattern of assistance with discrimination in the South prevailed in the Works Progress Administration. Executive orders prohibiting discrimination notwithstanding, local relief officials made it more difficult for blacks than whites to get on the WPA rolls and paid blacks less for the work-relief they performed than they did whites. By mid-1940, the fourteen southern and border states still had only eleven blacks among its more than ten thousand supervisors. Yet, the millions of dollars spent by the WPA for southern blacks meant survival, when even that had been in doubt. In 1938, some 140,000 black southerners worked on WPA projects. The following year, nearly three-quarters of a million black families in the South lived primarily on their WPA earnings. Indeed, the Works Progress Administration by the end of the 1930s rivaled both agriculture and domestic service as the chief source of black income in the South.[11]

The Public Works Administration also provided work-relief for the unemployed. Tightly run by Harold Ickes, a former president of the NAACP in Chicago, who insisted "that Congress intended this program to be carried out without discrimination," the PWA stipulated that all its construction contracts specify that the number of blacks hired and their percentage of the project payroll be equal to the proportion of blacks in the 1930 occupational census. Although sometimes disregarded by local officials and contractors, this quota resulted in unprecedented wages for southern black laborers and led to the admission of hundreds of blacks into previously all-white southern construction trade unions. It later led to similar quotas by the United States Housing Authority, the Federal Works Agency, and the President's Committee on Fair Employment Practices.

Due primiarly to Ickes's vigilance, moreover, blacks received 59 percent of the federally subsidized PWA and USHA housing in the South, and some $40 million in PWA funds went into the construction or renovation of over eight hundred hospitals, school buildings and libraries for southern blacks. This was a sum far, far greater than the federal government had spent for blacks during the seven decades after Emancipation.[12]

Following Ickes's lead, Aubrey Williams, the head of the National Youth Administration until its end in 1943, also made assistance to blacks one of his top priorities. Although the NYA accepted segregated projects in the South and employed a disproportionate number of southern blacks in servile work, Williams was attacked by white supremacists as a "nigger lover" and traitor to his native Alabama because he hired black administrative assistants to supervise Negro work in every southern state, forbade either geographical or racial differentials in wages, and insisted that Afro-American secondary and college students in every southern state receive aid at least in proportion to their numbers in the population. Still, the NYA helped only a minority of southern black youth who needed assistance. Despite Williams's fervor and the presence of more Afro-Americans in administrative posts in the NYA than in any other New Deal program, ably led by Mary McLeod Bethune, who headed the Office of Negro Affairs, the presence of proportionally far fewer black students than white in the South and the extremely limited scope of the out-of-school work program minimized the impact of the National Youth Administration.[13]

Similarly, despite the best of intentions toward Afro-Americans, the Resettlement Administration and the Farm Security Administration also barely scratched the surface of the needs of impoverished rural blacks in the South. The federal government's first "war on poverty" was simply overwhelmed by problems beyond its resources. Both Rexford Tugwell, chief of the RA, and Dr. Will Alexander, head of the FSA, showed real concern for southern blacks. Against determined opposition by the southern agricultural establishment and its spokesmen in Congress, even against the wishes of their own local committees in the South that administered RA and FSA programs, Tugwell and especially Alexander managed to insure benefits for black farmers roughly proportionate to their percentage of southern farm operators. But they could not prevent local committees from discriminating against blacks in the amount of loans awarded. And they could not force appropriations out of Congress to provide for more than a mere 1,393 black families on FSA resettlement communities by 1940. Even this minimal effort, however, earned the FSA a reputation as a "disturber of the peace," and a top place on the southern conservative's "death list" of New Deal agencies.[14]

Whether the New Deal could have done more to aid black southerners economically is problematic; the shortcomings of what it did are obvious. It never spent the kind of truly massive sums for relief that might have provided a new deal for those on the bottom rungs of the economic ladder. And, except for the

small minority of New Deal projects actually controlled by
officials in Washington, like the contracts for PWA construction, it
largely capitulated to local prejudice against blacks and allowed
racial discrimination in the administration of relief. The great
mass of black southerners remained in 1941, as they had been in
1933, victims of a brutally inequitable caste system. They continued to be mired in the ranks of menials, sharecroppers, unskilled laborers and domestics, twice as likely to be unemployed
as southern whites and earning only half the income of them
when they could find work.

Nevertheless, in no small part because of the economic assist-
ance that Afro-Americans did receive, blacks supported the New
Deal enthusiastically. They expressed their gratitude for New
Deal efforts to relieve black distress in letters to the White
House, in responses to interviewers, in lofty proclamations and
in earthy blues music, in how they voted and struggled to vote.
Black southerners who had never before received more than
crumbs eagerly accepted half a loaf. Despite receiving less aid
than they needed, the New Deal exceeded their expectations.
Hence, for the vast majority of southern blacks, the continuity of
discrimination seemed secondary to the significance of work-
relief, access to better housing, a government-sponsored health
clinic or infant care program, a federal program of part-time
employment so youths could stay in school, a FSA loan to purchase a farm, new recreational or educational facilities in the
neighborhood, a chance for vocational training or the opportunity
to learn to read and write in WPA literacy classes.[15]

Black southerners responded to the New Deal record on race
relations comparably, glorifying Roosevelt on the basis of what
they believed could be and has been rather than damning him on
a standard of what might be. They expected the leadership of
civil rights groups to criticize the president's failings yet, overall,
blacks judged FDR as far superior to past presidents on racial
matters. They credited him for taking political risks for blacks
and for defying white supremacists, however deficient his actual

effort to insure racial justice. Southern blacks well understood
the stiff resistance encountered by even racial moderation and
gradualism. Their expectations did not yet demand a frontal assault on Jim Crow, and the New Deal's limited immediate consequences seemed of less import than the implied promise of
change.[16]

In this spirit, blacks lauded the growing roster of Afro-
Americans working for the government. The number of blacks on
the federal payroll more than tripled during the depression decade, doubling the proportion of blacks in government jobs in the
1920s. Although most of the 150,000 black federal employees in
1941 worked in unskilled and semiskilled positions, New Dealers
unprecedently hired blacks as economists and engineers, as law-
yers and librarians, as scientists and office managers. Gunnar
Myrdal termed this novel development "the first significant step
toward the participation of Negros in federal government activity." And to prepare the way for future steps, the Roosevelt
Administration abolished the Civil Service regulations that had
required job-seekers to designate their race and to attach a photograph to their application forms. Numerous New Deal officials,
moreover, desegregated the cafeterias, restrooms, and secre-
tarial pools in their agencies and departments, further signifying
that black interests counted, that the Democratic constituency
included blacks, and that the New Deal sought—in Ralph
Bunche's words—"the full integration of the Negro into administrative government."[17]

The appointment of over a hundred blacks to administrative
posts in the New Deal proved an even more visible reminder of a
concern for Afro-American needs shown by no previous administration. Reversing two decades of diminishing black patronage,
Roosevelt elicited howls from his white southern supporters that
"Negroes were taking over the White House" by his selection of a
far larger number than ever before of race relations advisers in
formal government positions and his placement of them in positions of public importance so that both other government officials

and blacks regarded their presence as significant. Popularly referred to as the Black Cabinet or Black Brain Trust, these black
officials pushed for more equity in the relief and recovery programs and for greater concern by the Roosevelt Administration
on all issues of civil rights. They rarely succeeded. They never
possessed real power. But the very fact of such a large number of
black government officials, Roy Wilkins of the NAACP emphasized, "had never existed before." Their presence and prominence symbolized a New Deal effort to break with prevailing
customs of racial conservatism, as did Roosevelt's selection of
William Hastie as the first Afro-American federal judge in American history. In political language, such appointments meant that
blacks now mattered.[18]

So did the rhetoric and gestures of the Democratic party in
election years. To garner black votes, Roosevelt orchestrated a
series of precedent-shattering "firsts." Thirty black delegates attended the 1936 Democratic national convention. Never before
had the Democrats accredited an Afro-American as a delegate.
For the first time, moreover, the Democrats in 1936 invited
black reporters into the regular press box, chose a black minister
to offer the convention invocation, selected black politicians to
deliver the welcoming address and one of the speeches second-
ing Roosevelt's renomination, and even placed a Negro on the
delegation to notify Vice-President John Nance Garner of Texas
of his renomination. During the campaign, Roosevelt pointedly
promised that in his administration there would be "no forgotten
races" as well as no forgotten men. In 1940, the President publicly affirmed his administration's intention to include blacks fully
and fairly in defense training and employment, promoted the
first black to the army rank of brigadier general, and, for the first
time, included a specific Negro plank in the party platform,
pledging "to strive for complete legislative safeguards against
discrimination in government service and benefits and in the
national defense forces." Such political tokens promised more
than they delivered; but in the context of the times they had

significant impact in their future implications and in whetting the appetites of blacks for truly decisive government action. One consequence was the very significant increase in the size of the black electorate in the north during the Roosevelt era, and the mobilization of a large number of black southern organizations to promote voter registration and to arouse an interest in political participation among the masses of apathetic or apolitical blacks. [19]

The civil rights activities of members of Roosevelt's official family also implied change, gave hope, and raised racial expectations and consciousness. However much the president often remained outside the racial fray, he generally allowed those around him to plunge in. No previous administration had ever had so many prominent officials regularly conferring with black leaders, addressing the conventions of civil rights organizations, and declaring publicly for racial justice and equality. The racial statements and actions of Will Alexander, Harold Ickes, and Aubrey Williams repeatedly gained the plaudits of the Negro press and civil rights groups, as did those of W. Frank Persons of the Labor Department, Hallie Flanagan of the Federal Theatre Project, John M. Carmody of the Rural Electrification Administration, and Nathan Straus of the United States Housing Authority. Their outspoken advocacy of black rights helped make that issue a part of the liberal agenda and gave unprecedented official recognition to the plight of blacks. No administration had ever before devoted as much public attention to black needs, or expressed its sympathies so openly. [20]

The president's appointments to the Supreme Court, moreover, immediately and vitally affected the progress of black southerners toward full citizenship. With the exception of James Byrnes, Roosevelt's eight appointees proved to be true partisans of the civil rights cause. They began the dismantling of a century of law discriminating against blacks in their decisions involving the exclusion of blacks from juries, the right to picket against discrimination in employment, racial restrictive covenants, segregation in interstate transportation, peonage, disfranchisement, and discrimination in payment of black teachers and in graduate education. Their federalizing of the Bill of Rights left blacks less at the mercy of states' rights. Their expansion of the concept of state action severely circumscribed the permissable boundaries of private discrimination. And their insistence on inquiring into the facts of "separate but equal," rather than just the theory, diminished the possibility of segregation meeting the test of constitutionality. Accordingly, when the Supreme Court struck down the white primary of 1944, the only dissenter was the single justice then sitting whom Roosevelt had not appointed.[21]

Certainly no individual did more to encourage the hopefulness of black southerners than Mrs. Franklin Delano Roosevelt. She played the role of unofficial ombudsman for blacks, influenced her husband and other New Dealers to pay greater heed to the concerns of blacks, and prominently championed the civil rights cause. Repeatedly breaking with tradition, Eleanor Roosevelt openly hosted black receptions at the White House, posed for pictures with blacks, and associated herself with the major Negro and interracial groups of the decade. She supported the campaigns for antilynching and antipoll-tax legislation, and regularly promoted racial justice in public addresses, in her syndicated newspaper column, and in many published articles. At the opening session of the Southern Conference for Human Welfare in Birmingham, Alabama, in 1938, Mrs. Roosevelt defied the local segregation ordinance by conspicuously taking a seat on the "Colored" side of the auditorium. And when the Daughters of the American Revolution in 1939 would not permit its Constitution Hall to be used for a concert by a famous black contralto, Marian Anderson, Eleanor Roosevelt publicly decried the DAR's bigotry and resigned her membership, and then assisted the NAACP in arranging to hold the conference in front of the Lincoln Memorial. Throughout the Roosevelt era, the First Lady's actions stirred the wrath of the white South and emboldened southern blacks.[22]

While Franklin Roosevelt encouraged his wife to take certain public positions that he felt constrained to do, the president himself gradually assumed an egalitarian posture. With increasing frequency he invited blacks to the White House as guests and performers, appeared before black audiences, and conferred with civil rights leaders. He backed the movement to end all poll-tax requirements for voting, declaring that such taxes "are inevitably contrary to fundamental democracy and its representative form of government in which we believe." More cautiously, he condemned lynching and indicated his support for federal antilynching legislation. But he would never press for such a bill or try to thwart the filibusters by southern Democrats that kept the proposals from coming to a vote in the Senate. Most likely, nothing that FDR could have done would have secured antilynching legislation in the 1930s. The civil rights leadership understood this and acted accordingly. The president's pronouncements counted for more to them than his refusal to battle behind the scene. They recognized Roosevelt's need to mollify southern congressional leaders and the insurmountable barriers to cloture being voted. And they took heart from his establishment of a special Civil Rights Section of the Justice Department with power to investigate all lynchings that might involve some denial of a federal right.[23]

Perhaps most importantly, the reform spirit of the New Deal helped create a psychological climate in which black southerners and their allies could struggle with expectations of success. Real racial change began to seem a possibility. Often with presidential blessing, almost always with New Dealers playing a leading role, new reform movements in the South battled for racial justice. Southern liberals, nourished by Roosevelt and the New Deal, challenged the local power structures and forced the defenders of white supremacy on the defense. The "Silent South" grew vocal in its condemnation of racial discrimination and encouragement of black political consciousness. And black southerners responded with direct action campaigns against Jim Crow far greater in number than in any decade since Emancipation and which would not be surpassed until the 1960s. In boycotts and picket lines, marches and "sit-ins," southern blacks dramatically lobbied for civil rights legislation and protested against police brutality, cutbacks in relief appropriations, discrimination in employment and Jim Crow public facilities.[24]

"It is true that the millennium in race relations did not arrive under Roosevelt," the *Crisis* summed "but cynics and scoffers to the contrary, the great body of Negro citizens made progress." Blacks did not expect miracles in the Great Depression. They dared to hope for progress not perfection; and the intermixture of symbolic and substantive assistance, of rhetoric and recognition, swelled further hope in the formerly disheartened. Despite the fact that little had changed for the better in the concrete aspects of life for most black southerners, a belief that "we are on our way" took root. A new faith emerged. Blacks associated the New Deal with it, and idolized Franklin D. Roosevelt for it. A quarter of a century after his death, southern blacks would still be naming their children after FDR, and hanging his picture on the wall, more than that of any other public figure, white or black. Given the heritage of racism that shaped the political circumstances of the 1930s, they credited the New Deal with establishing government precedents favorable to blacks, with helping to end the "invisibility" of the race problem and make civil rights a part of the national liberal agenda, with generating reform and, as never before in our nation's history, propounding the federal government's responsibility in race relations. These changes did little to ameliorate the continuity of racism staining the New Deal, but they would help transform the despair, the discouragement, the dreadful apathy of black southerners into a fighting conviction of a better world that could soon and surely be achieved.[25]

The Era of the New Deal as a Turning Point in Southern History

NUMAN V. BARTLEY

Historians have traditionally regarded the American Civil War as the great turning point that divided the Old South from the New. According to standard interpretations, the war and the thirteenth amendment broke the political and social domination of planters and ushered in the leadership of businessmen and industrialists. Historical surveys of the New South rather consistently described the coming to power of new elites whose "values as well as purposes were bourgeois." They were, to quote another popular textbook on the New South, "of middle-class origin, having but nominal connections with the old planter regime and with primarily an industrial, capitalistic outlook."[1] Emancipation freed southern labor, and a new "modernizing" leadership assumed power. Southern developments reflected the kinds of changes in leadership and values associated with the industrial revolution in the North. Thus, southerners were much like other Americans, albeit Americans hampered by racial antagonisms, the sharecropping and furnishing systems, staple crop agriculture, educational deficiencies, and other problems.

This general scenario was not without substance, of course, but it also created interpretive difficulties. If social developments in the New South broadly parallelled those in the North, why did the South remain such a distinctive region? Why were non-southerners, as William Faulkner observed, so anxious to believe anything about the region "not even provided it be derogatory

but merely bizarre enough and strange enough."?² Whether it
was the "benighted South" of the 1920s, the nation's Number 1
economic problem of the 1930s, or the land of segregation and
violence during the post-World War II period, the region never
seemed to be in step with New Jersey, where it was presumably
supposed to be. Even after the decline of such quintessentially
southern practices as staple crop agriculture, sharecropping, and
institutionalized white supremacy, the region did not always live
up to national expectations. To explain this seeming paradox,
scholars frequently turned to psychological explanations and at-
tributed the South's failings, at least in part, to psychological
racism, mythology, romanticism, or similar phenomena.³ Thus,
traditional scholarship has tended to emphasize the importance
of the Civil War and its aftermath in restructuring southern leadership and outlook and has often offered psychological explanations for the region's unorthodox behavior.

Given these assumptions, scholars implicitly, if not always explicitly, treated the South as a stubbornly lagging North and
waited impatiently for urbanization and industrialization to
liberalize its people. During the post-World War II era, sym-
posia on the changing South became, in George B. Tindall's
words, "one of the flourishing minor industries of the region" and
often served as cheering sections for the region's "progress" toward national economic, demographic, and racial norms. To be
sure, a considerable number of historians, conscious of how many
times in the past southern distinctiveness had been prematurely
laid to rest, were unwilling to pronounce Dixie's epitaph, but
there was a general tendency to associate sectional convergence
with toleration in race relations and, in V. O. Key's words, "a
political system more completely in accord with the national
ideas of constitutional morality."⁴

More recent studies have challenged these assumptions.
Scholars of neo-Marxist persuasion have revitalized interest in
and to some extent have redefined the nature of class conflict and
accommodation in the New South, and they have directed atten-

tion to labor relations and ideology. Comparative history has led
to increasing recognition of the similarities between the South
and other underdeveloped areas and has resurrected the once
popular thesis that the New South suffered from its dependent
colonial relationship with the more advanced northern economy.
Studies in social history, particularly social histories of slavery,
have broadened the range of historical interest and have provided important insights into southern social structure and the
behavior of social groups. These trends in scholarship have produced a still somewhat hazy but quite different model of southern historical development.

Most notably, revisionist writers have minimized the disjunc-
tion caused by the Civil War. "Recent studies of politics, social
structure, and ideology after the Civil War," Eric Foner has
observed, "have been united by a single theme—continuity between the Old and New South."[5] This literature has failed to
substantiate the triumph of bourgeois elites during the era of the
Bourbons but instead has found evidence of planter persistence.
The Civil War did break the national power of southern planters,
but they remained the dominant social group in the South and
led the counterrevolution that overturned Reconstruction.
Emancipation transferred to black southerners sufficient bargaining power to force the breakup of antebellum labor practices, but
it did not eliminate coercive forms of labor control. The extent of
the ideological continuity between the Old South and the New
remains debatable, but recent studies have found that important
strands of ideological paternalism continued to influence regional
social behavior long after Appomattox and that racial proscription
contributed to a rigid social structure.

This literature at least offers a solution to one historiographical
controversy; it posits that the South was distinctive because it
was different. For the better part of a century after the Civil War,
the not-so-New South differed from the North in such fundamental ways as social structure, class composition, labor relations,
and ideology. Revisionist studies have also questioned the extent

to which psychological factors influence social behavior. Surely to a degree they do, and some of the works on romanticism, mythology, and the like have produced important insights, but, at the same time, it is no longer clear that psychological factors serve as independent variables. Recent studies strongly suggest that they are apt to gain currency when advanced and defended by powerful social groups. Finally, some revisionists argue that the South traveled a route to "modernization"—the Prussian Road—that was quite different from that taken in the North. Therefore, there was little reason to assume that southern urbanization, industrialization, and so on would produce the same results as did those developments in the North. Whatever the validity of Prussian Road theory, it does caution against the assumption that the South simply lagged behind the North.[6]

The purpose of this rather too lengthy and certainly too simplistic review of well-known historical literature has been to provide background for several generalizations—all of them broad and some of them quite tentative—about the course of modern southern history. The first and most obvious of these is of course the return to the tradition of Wilbur J. Cash and the reassertion of the continuity of late nineteenth and early twentieth-century southern history. While it would not be entirely appropriate to insist that nothing very important happened in the 1860s and the 1890s, those decades no longer seem, at least to me, to be the great watersheds that they have often been depicted. Instead, contemporary scholarship increasingly suggests that far more fundamental changes occurred during the middle years of the twentieth century, with perhaps 1935 to 1945 best qualifying as the latest crucial decade of New South historiography. Developments set in motion during these years produced massive changes in southern life.

Among the most fundamental was the breakdown of plantation agriculture. Despite Civil War and emancipation, the plantation was the South's basic economic and social institution and essentially remained so until the 1940s. Pete Daniel entitled a recent article not "The End of Slavery" but "The Metamorphosis of Slavery." Gilbert C. Fite concluded: "Farming throughout much of the South in the 1930s was little different than in the 1870s." Jack T. Kirby noted that the planters who "organized and dominated much of the flatland and hill South" transformed their plantations during the 1930s and 1940s into capitalist "neoplantations."[7] All three of these scholars—Daniel, Fite, and Kirby—have forthcoming book-length studies of southern agriculture that will undoubtedly broaden our understanding of these matters, but already it seems relatively clear that New Deal farm programs, mechanization, and other factors precipitated an upheaval in regional life. No longer was a country philosopher apt to observe that "as soon as a farmer begins to keep books, he'll go broke shore as hell."[8] Neoplantations kept books, and machines too, but they did not keep very many people.

The vast migration off the southern land was a fundamental demographic fact of the postdepression era. Between 1935 and 1970 more than thirteen million people left southern farms. During just the period from 1940 to 1945, more than 20 percent of the South's farm population abandoned agriculture. Both Daniel and Kirby have specifically, and in my opinion correctly, alluded to this massive exodus as a southern enclosure movement. In a traumatic kind of way, the process did more or less conform to contemporary theories of modernization. By 1930, the South had developed a dual economy of sorts, with the cities far more affluent and more "modern" than the poverty-stricken, "traditionalist" countryside, and "new ideas" did "spread outward" from the advanced "islands" to the backward areas.[9] The process, however, was hardly benign; it uprooted a rural people from the land and cast them into the nation's cities.

The upheaval disrupted the foundations of the southern social order. Tenancy and the furnishing system, race and sex, clan and class, and related arrangements defined proper social behavior. Labor relations were usually personal and often paternal as well as being exploitive and often coercive. These patterns carried over into other areas of southern enterprise, most notably in the case of the mill villages but also in mining villages, lumber and turpentine camps, and elsewhere. This system of labor relations appeared in such odd areas as shrimp fishing, where shrimpers sometimes lived in company houses, sailed company boats, received company credit, and fished on shares. "Crewmen gets everything furnished and the factory gets a share of the shrimp," a shrimper explained to a WPA interviewer. "Working on a factory boat is like being a share cropper."[10]

The network of dependency relationships was a basic feature of the southern work place. In the 1890s Edward Atkinson, a Boston textile magnate, observed that southern industrial promoters thought in terms of a large textile factory constructed largely with imported capital and operated in part by skilled workmen enticed from Massachusetts. Actually, Atkinson explained, healthy industrial growth was "a single great factory surrounded by a hundred little work shops." The lack of the "hundred little work shops" was a severe impediment to economic growth, and Atkinson's explanation for this absence was that the "idea of caste and class still prevails" in the region.[11] With regard to capitalist development, Atkinson was precisely accurate. The "single great factory" did not threaten social stability and the patriarchal order; the "hundred little work shops" suggested a free-labor capitalism and a more dynamic social system that might threaten the "idea of caste and class." Although buttressed by a paternalistic ideology that encompassed the cult of the Lost Cause and other mythologies, the system ultimately rested on the bedrock of white supremacy, which helps to explain why virtually all establishment spokesmen placed defense of white supremacy above all other public and political virtues.

The South was by no means static, of course, and by the 1920s the growing cities nurtured an increasingly self-confident "business-oriented middle class" anxious to encourage what Blaine A. Brownell has called "the urban ethos in the South."[12] Numerous other town and city dwellers and yeomen farmers did not live in company houses or shop on credit at company stores. Nevertheless, southerners generally were caught up in the web of marketing and credit arrangements that were a part of the South's colonial dependence on the North and were influenced by the prevailing regional commitment to social stability and a hierarchical order. W. J. Cash had a definite point when he described the southern factory as "a plantation, essentially indistinguishable in organization from the familiar plantation of the cotton fields."[13] At any rate, New Deal wage and hours legislation, World War II economic expansion, and changing social conditions consigned factory communities to approximately the same fate as tenant farmers.

The enclosure movement in agriculture and the passing of the relatively self-contained workers' villages along with the decline of isolation and provincialism generally freed southern labor to flow unhindered in response to market forces. The result was not free labor, at least not as that term has been defined by Eric Foner and others.[14] Instead, the collapse of paternal forms of labor control—and the word collapse is fitting despite the fact that the change extended over several decades—spurred the creation of what might best be termed commodity labor. Karl Polanyi described the central features of a commodity labor system, albeit in a highly critical manner: "To separate labor from other activities of life and to subject it to the laws of the market was to annihilate all organic forms of existence and to replace them by a different type of organization, an atomistic and individualistic one."[15] The southern work place became depersonalized and possibly dehumanized while at the same time it became less coercive and possibly less exploitive. The behavior of southern working people changed, and so too did southern society's attitudes toward work.

The decline of ideological paternalism encouraged an expanding commitment to economic growth. The urban boosterism of the 1920s gained momentum after the depression of the 1930s had exposed the bankruptcy of southern agriculture. The state planning agencies funded by the New Deal quickly evolved into industrial promotion boards, and in 1936 Mississippi established its Balance Agriculture With Industry program. Thereafter, all of the southern states created industrial development commissions and, as James C. Cobb has demonstrated, competed vigorously with a variety of programs and policies designed to offer favors and services to national and international corporations that chose to expand into the South.[16] Southern assistance to corporate enterprise was sufficiently generous to perhaps justify a wag's remark that the South believed in "socialism for the rich and free enterprise for the poor." By 1964 Leslie W. Dunbar of the Southern Regional Council could appropriately muse: "Southern governors have become the de facto executive directors of the state chambers of commerce, and spend their time competing with each other as supplicants for new plants. We have talked of state socialism and state capitalism, but what do we call governments whose chief affair it is to entice and propitiate business?"[17]

Whatever the answer to Dunbar's question, the economic growth ethos came to dominate the formulation of southern state policy. Changes within southern society and most directly the black civil rights movement made institutionalized white supremacy no longer compatible with social order and led prevailing elites to identify social harmony with more factory payrolls and office parks. As the locus of southern political and economic power shifted from plantation-oriented county seats to corporation-oriented metropolitan areas, economic expansion came to be championed as the panacea for southern public problems.

This outlook, incidentally, coincided with the changing views of northern elites. In 1938 the Roosevelt administration released its *Report on Economic Conditions of the South*, which was a sound summary of the region's economic disasters. The *Report* associated virtually all of these debilities with the South's colonial dependency relationship with the North. President Roosevelt's covering letter declared the region to be "the Nation's No. 1 economic problem—the Nation's problem, not merely the

South's."[18] The document symbolized shifts in federal policies
that made the national government a significant sponsor of southern economic growth. Northern liberal journals, one study has
reported, tended to agree with this assessment and to favor federal aid to the South. Although the *Report* for a time made
national liberals suspicious of private economic penetration of a
colonized region, the dominant view soon came to be that northern corporate expansion into the region was the best solution to
southern "backwardness."[19] Thus, for much of the post-World
War II era, southern elites and northern liberals were in essential agreement that northern corporate enterprise would solve
southern problems.

The expansion of northern enterprise into the South and the
growth of federal programs supporting southern "progress" contributed to the depopulation of rural areas and the growth of
cities and factories. Commodity labor replaced the more personal
labor relations of an earlier era and a growth-oriented metropolitan elite replaced a county-seat elite committed to traditional
social stability. Such upheavals led to profound and as yet ill-
understood changes in social structures, ideology, and personal
interrelationships.

During much of the post-World War II period, academicians
tended to interpret these developments from the perspective of
growing per capita incomes, rising cities and factories, and expanding educational facilities and to applaud southern progress
while often expressing dismay over the reluctance of many southerners—especially rural and working-class white southerners—
to accept these gains. More recently scholars have evidenced
greater sensitivity to the price of "progress." Like a Faulknerian
novel, the southern success story was also a tale of "the disinte-
gration of a family, of a tradition, and of a culture."[20]

Community, family, religion, place, and other traditional
southern verities declined, and the recent tendency has been to
view these changes from a critical perspective. Students of southern intellectual history have described the triumph of modern-

ism, which in addition to its other virtues also seems to have been a victory for situational ethics and relativist morality. Richard H. King has examined "the cultural awakening of the American South" during the period 1930–55 and has depicted the emergence of a society that "lacks any compelling vision to unite its members beyond the dictates of self-interest."[21] As a novelist pointed out, "Friendship is a luxury. Unless you're so poor it makes no difference how you spend your time."[22] The depopulation of the countryside and the breakup of the mill villages contributed to the divorce of work from family, which modernization theorists assure us also encourages "the separation of morals from economics."[23] Journalists decried the southern lust for economic growth that was making the region "etherized in all those ways a people are subtly rendered pastless, memoryless, blank of identity, by assimilation into chrome and asphalt and plastic."[24] Even Erskine Caldwell, now that Tobacco Road was paved and Jeeter Lester's cotton field was part of a cattle farm, stated that "people are no better off in the city than they were in the country—and probably worse off."[25] This literature suggests that the price of progress was high indeed.

Southerners became more like other Americans but at the same time the "modernization" of the South took place in a different era and under different historical conditions than it did in the North. Southern industrial promoters pointedly directed their efforts toward attracting outside investments, not toward the creation of a homemade New South with internally generated capital. Whether or not the South remained in something akin to a state of colonial dependency, investors from outside the region still dominated much of the southern economy. A recent article in an Atlanta business publication entitled "Who Owns Atlanta?" revealed rather pridefully that "most of the prime properties in town are controlled by interests headquartered elsewhere: New York, Dallas, Boston, Toronto, Hamburg, Amsterdam, Al Kuwait."[26] On a broader scale this finding illustrates a basic feature of southern urban and economic growth.

Southern urbanization took place within a "regional framework" that differed from the northern urbanizing experience,[27] and southern industrialization resulted in significant measure from the desire of northern corporate elites to escape labor unions and high taxes. These developments contributed to the growth of free market individualism, but they did not noticeably encourage political liberalism. Southern elites consistently demonstrated a propensity to favor public aid for industrialists, to oppose labor organization, to support relatively low taxes and services, and to tailor social policies to the needs of land developers and real estate brokers. Such findings led James Cobb, the leading student of southern industrial promotion, to conclude that these policies were based on "a philosophy of development that insured restricted growth and confirmed rather than threatened established power relationships."[28] Also noteworthy is the fact that southern promoters of urban and industrial progress had largely accomplished their goal before the civil rights movement and federal legislation forced equality—or more correctly the legal symbols of equality—in the marketplace. Certainly the persistence of poverty, racism, and a variety of other social ailments testifies to the failure of economic growth to solve southern social problems.

If I read this literature correctly, it would appear that many observers longed for the South to join the mainstream of national life. Having seen that goal to some degree achieved, they, like Will Herberg's Catholics and Jews, have tended to become suspicious of sectional convergence. In 1957 Flannery O'Connor wrote: "The anguish that most of us have observed for some time now has been caused not by the fact that the South is alienated from the rest of the country, but by the fact that it is not alienated enough, that every day we are getting more and more like the rest of the country, that we are being forced out, not only of our many sins but of our few virtues."[29] This sentiment has become more widespread among articulate southerners. John Shelton Reed, in his most recent study of southern attitudes, found regional consciousness (though not traditional regional values) greatest among urban, educated, "sophisticated" southerners.[30] Such intellectual currents influenced scholars who study the South as well no doubt as did the tawdry results achieved from the region's promotion from nation's number one economic problem to the sunbelt South.

This healthy contemporary scepticism about southern "progress" has produced fruitful scholarship but it also runs the danger of falling victim to what Reinhard Bendix has called the "romantic fallacy."[31] Despite the strengths of traditional southern culture, that society was wracked by poverty, disease, and white supremacy. If the changes in southern life are measured in material terms, which until recently was what scholars normally did, then the word progress is not at all inappropriate. Not only were southerners more affluent during the post-World War II years than they had ever been before, but the opportunities for economic advancement were greater for white males than at any time since the building of the cotton kingdom in the early nineteenth century and for other southerners greater than at any time in the past. The breakdown of the paternal order generated an expansion of individualism—as limited, atomistic, and legalistic as that individualism was—that underlay the civil rights movement as well as the expanding role of women in southern society. Being governed by a leadership oriented toward the corporate boardrooms of Atlanta, Dallas, and New York may even have some advantages over being governed by county-seat elites and their New York creditors. These gains were achieved at high cost to the South's people and their environment, and the coming of a system of labor relations that impersonally treats people as commodities does not yet appear to have improved the quality of southern life. A comprehensive evaluation of the changes that grew from the upheavals of the 1930s and 1940s is yet to be accomplished, but it does seem to me that students of southern history are rapidly moving toward a much clearer base from which to start.

Notes

Notes to INTRODUCTION
by James C. Cobb and Michael V. Namorato

1. Wilbur J. Cash, *The Mind of the South* (New York: Alfred A. Knopf, 1941).
2. C. Vann Woodward, *Origins of the New South, 1877–1913* (Baton Rouge: Louisiana State University Press, 1951).
3. Jonathan M. Wiener, *The Social Origins of the New South* (Baton Rouge: Louisiana State University Press, 1978).
4. Dwight B. Billings, Jr., *Planters and the Making of a New South* (Chapel Hill: University of North Carolina Press, 1979).
5. The legacy of the postbellum economic and racial adjustment is described in Roger L. Ransom and Richard Sutch, *One Kind of Freedom: The Economic Consequences of Emancipation,* (London: Cambridge University Press, 1977).
6. Ralph McGill, *The South and the Southerner* (Boston: Little Brown, 1963).
7. George B. Tindall, *The Emergence of the New South, 1913–1945* (Baton Rouge, Louisiana State University Press, 1967).
8. I. A. Newby, *The South: A History* (New York: Holt, Rinehart and Winston, 1978).
9. Frank Freidel, *F.D.R. and the South* (Baton Rouge: Louisiana State University Press, 1965).
10. Pete Daniel, "The Transformation of the Rural South, 1930 to the Present," *Agricultural History,* 55 (July 1981), 231–48.
11. F. Ray Marshall, *Labor in the South* (Cambridge, Mass.: Harvard University Press, 1967).
12. Raymond Wolters, Jr., *Negroes and the Great Depression* (Westport, Conn.: Greenwood Press, 1970).
13. Harvard Sitkoff, *A New Deal for Blacks* (New York: Oxford University Press, 1978).
14. Numan V. Bartley, *The Rise of Massive Resistance* (Baton Rouge: Louisiana State University Press, 1969).
15. William N. Parker, "The South in the National Economy, 1865–1970," *Southern Economic Journal* 46 (April 1980), 1019–48.

Notes to *THE SOUTH AND THE NEW DEAL*
by Frank Freidel

1. Herbert Stein at session on FDR, American Historical Association, December 1982. The indispensable survey of almost all facets of the New Deal in the South is George Tindall, *The Emergence of the New South, 1913–1945* (Baton Rouge: Louisiana State University Press, 1967) chs. 11–19. These brief notes do not indicate my considerable indebtedness to a number of authors of fine monographs and articles on southern history during the New Deal period. To cite them all would make the notes almost as long as the text.

2. Minnie Fisher Cunningham to Dorothy Kirchwey Brown, [after July 28, 1928], Brown mss., Schlesinger Library, Radcliffe College.

3. FDR, PPA, 1934: 273–274; *Time*, vol. 32, July 11, 1938.

4. Daniel J. Singal, *The War Within* (Chapel Hill: University of North Carolina Press, 1982); Morton Sosna, *In Search of the Silent South* (New York: Columbia University Press, 1977); and Tindall, *Emergence of the New South* develop these themes.

5. Bascom Timmons, *Garner of Texas* (New York: Harper, 1948), 165–66. On Roosevelt, see Frank Freidel, *FDR and the South* (Baton Rouge: Louisiana State University Press, 1965).

6. Charles W. Eagles, *Jonathan Daniels and Race Relations* (Knoxville: University of Tennessee Press, 1982).

7. Rexford G. Tugwell interview with Eleanor Roosevelt, June 24, 1957, Warm Springs Foundation.

8. James P. Louis, "Sue Shelton White," in Edward T. James and others, eds., *Notable American Women, 1607–1950* (Cambridge, Mass.: Belknap Press of Harvard University Press, 1971), 3:590–592; Susan Ware, *Beyond Suffrage* (Cambridge, Mass.: Harvard University Press, 1981).

9. Leon H. Keyserling interview, January 9, 1969, Lyndon B. Johnson Library; Katie Louchheim, ed., *The Making of the New Deal* (Cambridge, Mass.: Harvard University Press, 1983), 196.

10. Virginia Hamilton, interview with Thad Holt, October 1974; Holt, "Memorandum on the Development of Agencies for Work Relief under the New Deal"; Holt, "Establishment of Unemployment Relief Agencies in the Hoover-Roosevelt Era," History Department, University of Alabama, Birmingham.

11. Tindall, *The Emergence of the New South*, pp. 460, 471–72.

12. John Nance Garner to FDR, June 20, 1937; Harry Hopkins to FDR, June 2, 1937, and enclosures, PPF 1416, FDR mss.

13. Martha H. Swain, *Pat Harrison: The New Deal Years* (Jackson: University Press of Mississippi, 1978); John Bankhead to Marie Bankhead Owen, April 20, 1939, J. H. Bankhead mss., Alabama Archives.

14. Fred M. Vinson to W. B. Bankhead, October 2, 1936; Bankhead to Vinson, October 7, 1936, W. B. Bankhead mss., Alabama Archives.

15. National Emergency Council, *Report on Economic Conditions of the South* (Washington, D.C., Government Printing Office, 1938); Tindall, *The Emergence of the New South*, 598–599.

16. See for example, Paul E. Mertz, *New Deal Policy and Southern Rural Poverty* (Baton Rouge: Louisiana State University Press, 1978); John D. Minton, *The New Deal in Tennessee, 1932–1938* (New York: Garland Pub. Inc., 1979); Sidney Baldwin, *Poverty and Politics: The Rise and Decline of the Farm Security*

Administration (Chapel Hill: University of North Carolina Press, 1968); and Paul K. Conkin, *Tomorrow a New World: The New Deal Community Program* (Ithaca, N.Y., Cornell University Press, 1959).

17. Studs Terkel, *Hard Times* (New York: Pantheon Books, 1970), 530–531.

18. Louchheim, ed., *The Making of the New Deal*, xvii–xviii.

Notes to THE NEW DEAL, SOUTHERN AGRICULTURE, AND ECONOMIC CHANGE
by Pete Daniel

1. Virginius Dabney, *Below the Potomac: A Book about the New South* (New York: D. Appleton Century, 1942), 59.

2. William Faulkner, *The Town* (New York: Random House, 1957), 245.

3. "Concentration of Control of Agricultural Land," n.d., Land Tenure Section, Bureau of Agricultural Economics, Record Group 83, National Archives (Hereafter cited BAE, RG 83, NA); Harold C. Larsen, "Farm-Mortgage Investments of Life Insurance Companies," 1943, Manuscripts, 1940–46, ibid.; Harold T. Lingard, "Lender Distribution of Farm-Mortgage Recordings, 1910–39," *Agricultural Finance Review* 3 (May 1940), 23–30, copy in Box 16, Records of the Temporary National Economic Committee, Record Group 144, National Archives (Hereafter cited TNEC, RG 144, NA); Douglas Helms, "Just Lookin' for a Home: The Cotton Boll Weevil and the South," (Ph.D. diss., Florida State University, 1977); James H. Shideler, *Farm Crisis: 1919–1923* (Berkeley: University of California Press, 1957); Gilbert C. Fite, "Voluntary Attempts to Reduce Cotton Acreage in the South, 1914–1933," *Journal of Southern History* 14 (Nov. 1948), 481–99; Robert E. Snyder, "The Cotton Holiday Movement in Mississippi, 1931," *Journal of Mississippi History* 40 (Feb. 1978), 1–32; Henry I. Richards, *Cotton and the AAA* (Washington, D.C.: The Brookings Institution, 1936); Pete Daniel, *Deep'n as it Come: The 1927 Mississippi River Flood* (New York: Oxford University Press, 1977); Nan E. Woodruff, "The Failure of Relief During the Arkansas Drought of 1930–31," *Arkansas Historical Quarterly* 39 (Winter 1980), 301–13.

4. "You're Gonna Have Lace Curtains," Federal Writers Project *These Are Our Lives* (New York: Norton, 1975. Orig. pub. in 1939), 11.

5. E. F. Hobsbaum and George Rude, *Captain Swing* (New York: Norton, 1975).

6. David Eugene Conrad, *The Forgotten Farmers: The Story of Sharecroppers in the New Deal* (Urbana: University of Illinois Press, 1965); Donald H. Grubbs, *Cry from the Cotton: The Southern Tenant Farmers' Union and the New Deal* (Chapel Hill: University of North Carolina Press, 1971); H. L. Mitchell, *Mean Things Happening in this Land: The Life and Times of H. L. Mitchell, Cofounder of the Southern Tenant Farmers Union* (Montclair, N.J.: Allanheld, Osmun & Co., 1979); Paul E. Mertz, *New Deal Policy and Southern Rural Poverty* (Baton Rouge: Louisiana State University Press, 1978); Sidney Baldwin, *Poverty and Politics: The Rise and Decline of the Farm Security Administration* (Chapel Hill: University of North Carolina Press, 1968). "If Tugwell had launched his Resettlement Administration in 1933," Paul Conkin concluded, "he probably would have achieved many of his goals without serious congressional opposition," Paul Conkin, *Tomorrow a New World: The New Deal Community Program*

(Ithaca: Cornell University Press, 1959), 330.

7. FERA, Division of Research and Statistics, Harold Hoffsommer, Survey of Rural Problem Areas, Cotton Growing Region of the South, Franklin County, North Carolina, BAE, RG 83, NA.

8. Maynard P. West to Thomas G. Burch, Sept. 13, 1933, Agricultural Adjustment Administration, Tobacco, Record Group 145, National Archives. (Hereafter cited AAA, commodity, RG 145, NA).

9. Lowe to Henry A. Wallace and Charles Miller, April 29, 1935; Lowe to Wallace, May 7, 1935, Rice, Records of the Secretary of Agriculture, Record Group 16, National Archives (Hereafter cited SOA, RG 16, NA). See also, Hubert C. Wirtz to Allen Ellender, Dec. 29, 1955; Isaac Guillory to Russell Long, Jan. 30, 1956, Rice, AAA, RG 145, NA.

10. Frank Freidel, *F. D. R. and the South* (Baton Rouge: Louisiana State University Press, 1965), 10–14.

11. FERA, Division of Research and Statistics, Harold Hoffsommer, Survey of Rural Problem Areas, Cotton Growing Region of the Old South, Meriwether County, Georgia, BAE, RG 83, NA.

12. Dan T. Hammil, et al., to J. B. Hutson, Sept. 23, 1933, A. L. Jones to Hugh S. Johnson, Sept. 15, 1933, Tobacco, AAA, RG 145, NA.

13. Nick Tosches, *Hellfire: The Jerry Lee Lewis Story* (New York: Delacorte Press, 1983), 21–22.

14. Glen T. Barton and J. G. McNeeley, "Recent Changes in Labor Organization on Arkansas Plantations," Land Tenure Section, Box 1030, BAE, RG 83, NA.

15. Anthony J. Badger, *Prosperity Road: The New Deal, Tobacco, and North Carolina* (Chapel Hill: University of North Carolina Press, 1980).

16. Rudolph Carrol Hammack, "The New Deal and Louisiana Agriculture," (Ph.D. diss., Tulane University, 1973); Unsigned memorandum for the Secretary, March 19, 1935, Rice, SOA, RG 16, NA; J. W. Bateman to Henry A. Wallace, Jan. 8, 1935; "Announcement, 1935 Adjustment Program for Southern Rice," March 19, 1935; Charles B. Howe, memorandum to William E. Byrd, March 12, 1936, Rice, AAA, RG 145, NA; "Legislative History of the De Rouen Amendment," Rice Millers Papers, Box 1, University of Southwestern Louisiana.

17. Huey Long, Radio Address, 1935; Address, WABC, Feb. 10, 1935, Library of Congress.

18. Kenneth D. Yielding and Paul H. Carlson, compl., *Ah That Voice: The Fireside Chats of Franklin Delano Roosevelt* (Odessa, Texas: John H. Shepperd, Jr., Library of the Presidents, Presidential Museum, 1974); Robert S. Fine, "Roosevelt's Radio Chatting: Its Development and Impact During the Great Depression," (Ph.D. diss., New York University, 1977); Charles Grant Curtis, Jr., "Franklin D. Roosevelt and the Commonwealth of Broadcasting," (Honors Thesis, Harvard College, 1978).

19. U.S. Congress, Senate, *Payments Under Agricultural Adjustment Program*, S. Doc. 274, 74 Cong., 2 Sess., 1936, 34–58; FERA, Division of Research and Statistics, Harold Hoffsommer, Survey of Rural Problem Areas, Cotton Growing Region of the Old South, Leflore County, Mississippi, 6, BAE, RG 83, NA.

20. *Payments Under Agricultural Adjustment Program*, 94–95; Arthur M. Collens to J. B. Hutson, Sept. 25, 1933; Glen T. Rogers to Hutson, Jan. 19, 1934, Tobacco, AAA, RG 145, NA.

21. *Payments Under Agricultural Adjustment Program*, 11, 68–71.

22. Moses Senkumba Musoke, "Mechanizing Cotton Production in the American South: The Tractor, 1915–1960," *Explorations in Economic History* 18 (1981),

356. For an overview of mechanization, see Musoke, "Technical Change in Cotton Production in the United States, 1925–1960," (Ph.D. diss., University of Wisconsin, Madison, 1976).

23. David Wayne Ganger, "The Impact of Mechanization and the New Deal's Acreage Reduction Programs on Cotton Farmers during the 1930s," (Ph.D. diss., University of California, Los Angeles, 1973), 360–61, 401–2, 405–6.

24. J. C. Elrod, D. E. Young, and W. T. Fullilove, "Farm Rental Arrangements in Georgia," Manuscripts, 1940–46, BAE, RG 83, NA. See also, J. C. Elrod, "Types of Tenancy Areas in Georgia," Land Tenure Section, ibid.

25. Glen T. Barton and J. G. McNeeley, "Recent Changes in Labor Organization on Arkansas Plantations," Land Tenure Section, ibid. See also, Donald C. Alexander, *The Arkansas Plantation, 1920–1942* (New Haven: Yale University Press, 1943), 79, 86–87.

26. U.S. Congress, Senate, Special Committee to Investigate Unemployment and Relief, Feb. 28–April 8, 1938, Testimony of Paul S. Taylor, 1158, 1161, 75 Cong., 3 Sess., copy in Statistics and History, BAE, RG 83, NA.

27. Ibid. See also, "Testimony before the TNEC on Human and Socio-Economic Effects of Displacement in Agriculture," testimony of Paul S. Taylor, Box 34, TNEC, RG 144, NA; "Plan for Cooperation between Rural Rehabilitation Division of the FERA and the AAA in Handling cases of eviction of Tenants and Sharecroppers on Account of Inability of Landlords to Finance Them," May 27, 1935, Cotton, AAA, RG 145, NA; Richard H. Day, "The Economics of Technological Change and the Demise of the Sharecropper," *The American Economic Review* 57 (June 1967), 427–49.

28. On this theme, see Carroll W. Pursell, Jr., "Government and Technology in the Great Depression," *Technology and Culture* 20 (Jan. 1979), 162–74.

29. Marshall Harris in the Bureau of Agricultural Economics collected material on how to reform the southern tenure system. See, "Report on Compensation as a Means of Improving the Farm Tenancy System," Nov. 1936; "Compensation for Improvement, Deterioration, and Disturbance in Landlord-Tenant Relations," July 1935, Land Tenure Section, BAE, RG 83, NA.

Notes to THE NEW DEAL AND SOUTHERN LABOR
by J. Wayne Flynt

1. Florence Reece, "Which Side Are You On?", *Southern Exposure*, 4 (Spring/ Summer 1976), 90.

2. Irving Bernstein, *Turbulent Years: A History of the American Worker, 1933–1941* (Boston: Houghton Mifflin Company, 1970), pp. 323–342.

3. Ibid., p. 770.

4. Ibid., p. 771, and James H. Hodges, "The New Deal Labor Policy and the Southern Textile Industry, 1933–1941," Ph.D. dissertation, Vanderbilt University, 1963.

5. See Selig Perlman, "Labor and the New Deal in Historical Perspective," *Labor and the New Deal*, Milton Derber and Edwin Young, eds. (Madison, Wisconsin: The University of Wisconsin Press, 1957).

6. Bernstein adopts the dates 1933–1941, and Walter Galenson, *The CIO Challenge to the AFL: A History of the American Labor Movement, 1935–1941* (Cambridge: Harvard University Press, 1960), used the same basic chronology in

an earlier work.

7. See David Brody "Labor and The Great Depression: The Interpretive Prospects," *Labor History*, 13 (Spring 1972). This is an excellent summary of current interpretive positions.

8. See Christopher L. Tomlins, "AFL Unions in the 1930's: Their Performance in Historical Perspective", *The Journal of American History*, 65 (March 1979), 1021–1042.

9. See Ronald Radosh, "The Corporate Ideology of American Labor Leaders from Gompers to Hillman," *For A New America: Essays in History and Politics from Studies on the Left, 1959–1967*, James Weinstein and David W. Eakins, eds. (New York: Random House, 1970).

10. Brody, "Labor and The Great Depression," pp. 233–235.

11. F. Ray Marshall, *Labor in the South* (Cambridge: Harvard University Press, 1967), p. 139.

12. See John W. Hevener, *Which Side Are You On? The Harlan County Coal Miners, 1931–1939* (Urbana: University of Illinois Press, 1978).

13. Thomas C. Longin, "Coal, Congress and the Courts: The Bituminous Coal Industry and The New Deal," *West Virginia History*, 35 (January 1974), 101–130.

14. President, U.M.W., Hull Coal Mining Camp to President Franklin D. Roosevelt, October 7, 1933, Copy in "Correspondence File, 1930–1935," Philip Taft Research Notes, Archives, Birmingham Public Library. Hereafter cited as Taft Papers.

15. C. L. Richardson to H. L. Kerwin, August 21, 1933, copy in "Correspondence File, 1930–35," Taft Papers.

16. William Mitch to Hugh L. Kerwin, August 8, 1933, copy in "Correspondence File, 1930–35," Taft Papers.

17. Charles Edmundson to H. L. Kerwin, March 21, 1934, copy in "Correspondence File, 1930–35," Taft Papers.

18. Marshall, *Labor in the South*, pp. 143–144.

19. William Mitch to Francis Perkins, August 3, 1934, and Mitch to H. L. Kerwin, September 30, 1935, "Correspondence File, 1930–35," Taft Papers.

20. Marshall, *Labor in the South*, p. 141.

21. Hevener, *Which Side Are You On?*, p. 181.

22. Galenson, *The CIO Challenge to the AFL*, pp. 89–96.

23. Marshall, *Labor in the South*, pp. 186–188.

24. Charles H. Martin, "Southern Labor Relations in Transition: Gadsden Alabama, 1930–1943", *The Journal of Southern History*, 47 (November 1981), 548.

25. Ibid., 559–560.

26. Daniel Nelson, "A CIO Organizer in Alabama, 1941," *Labor History*, 18 (Fall 1977), 579.

27. Ibid., 584.

28. Bernstein, *Turbulent Years*, pp. 616–617; Hodges, "The New Deal Labor Policy and the Southern Textile Industry, 1933–1941", pp. 25, 27, 33–35.

29. Hodges, "The New Deal Labor Policy and the Southern Textile Industry, 1933–1941," pp. 60, 64.

30. Ibid., pp. 60, 104.

31. George H. Van Fleet to H. L. Kerwin, Department of Labor, April 10, 1930, copy in "Correspondence File, 1930–35," Taft Papers.

32. C. L. Richardson to H. L. Kerwin, June 8, 1933, copy in "Correspondence File, 1930–35," Taft Papers.

33. "Settlement of Strike in Kendall Mills, Newberry, S.C.", October 23, 1933,

United Textile Workers of America Papers, Southern Labor Archives, Georgia State University, Atlanta. Hereafter cited as UTWA Papers, Southern Labor Archives.

34. "Report and Recommendations of the Cotton Textile Work Assignment Board to President Franklin D. Roosevelt For a Permanent Plan for Regulation of Work Assignments in the Cotton Textile Industry," May, 1935. Copy in UTWA Papers, Southern Labor Archives.

35. Hodges, "The New Deal Labor Policy and the Southern Textile Industry, 1933–1941," pp. 250, 254.

36. Ibid., p. 326.

37. Witherspoon Dodge, "Free Enterprise," unpublished manuscript in Stetson Kennedy Papers, Southern Labor Archives.

38. Hodges, "The New Deal Labor Policy and the Southern Textile Industry, 1933–1941," quoted on p. 126.

39. Ibid., pp. 469–470.

40. See James S. Olson, "Organized Black Leadership and Industrial Unionism: The Racial Response, 1936–1945," Labor History, 10 (Summer 1969), 475–486.

41. See Michael S. Holmes, "The Blue Eagle as 'Jim Crow Bird': The NRA and Georgia's Black Workers", The Journal of Negro History, 57 (July 1972), 276–283.

42. George W. Whitaker to Francis Perkins, December 21, 1933; H. L. Kerwin to George W. Whitaker, December 27, 1933; copies in "Correspondence File, 1930–35," Taft Papers.

43. Marshall, Labor in the South, pp. 150–152.

44. Groesbeck Parham and Gwen Robinson, "If I Could Go Back. . . ," Southern Exposure, 4 (Spring/Summer 1976), 16–20.

45. Larry Rogin, "Labor Education: Uneasy Beginnings," and Myles Horton, "The Spark That Ignites," Southern Exposure, 4 (Spring/Summer 1976), pp. 150–153, and pp. 153–156.

46. Martin, "Southern Labor Relations in Transition," 554.

47. John D. House, "Report on Violations of Civil Liberties in Gadsden, Alabama," n.d., United Rubber Workers Local No. 12, Gadsden, Alabama, Southern Labor Archives.

48. Marshall, Labor in the South, p. 144.

49. Jerold S. Auerbach, Labor and Liberty: The LaFollette Committee and the New Deal (Indianapolis and New York: The Bobbs-Merrill Co., 1966), pp. 116–117.

50. Ibid., p. 118.

51. Ibid., pp. 117–120.

52. Eli Futch to Joe ?, June 11, 1934; R. L. Glenn to Duncan U. Fletcher, June 11, 1934; in Park Trammell Papers, P. K. Yonge Library of Florida History, University of Florida. Interview with Representative Claude Pepper, September 1, 1964, Washington, D.C.

53. Robert R. Moore (President, Alabama State Federation of Labor) to William O. Hare (Secretary-Treasurer, Alabama State Federation of Labor), June 5, 1934; and Robert R. Moore to Members of the Alabama Legislative, June 19, 1935; Taft Papers.

54. Wayne Flynt, "A Vignette in Southern Labor Politics—The 1936 Mississippi Senatorial Primary," Mississippi Quarterly: The Journal of Southern Culture, 26 (Winter 1972–'73), 89–99.

55. John E. Allen, "Eugene Talmadge and the Great Textile Strike in Georgia,

September, 1934," in Gary M. Fink and Merl E. Reed, eds., *Essays in Southern Labor History*, (Westport, Connecticut: Greenwood Press, 1976), pp. 224–243.

56. Noel R. Beddow to Donald R. Richberg, April 15, 1935, Copy in "Correspondence File, 1930–35," Taft Papers.

57. Daniel A. Powell, "PAC to COPE: Thirty-Two Years of Southern Labor in Politics," *Essays in Southern Labor History*, pp. 224, 247, 254.

58. George N. Green, "Anti-Labor Politics in Texas, 1941–1957," *American Labor in the Southwest: The First One Hundred Years*, James C. Foster, editor (Tucson, Arizona: The University of Arizona Press, 1982), p. 220.

59. Powell, "PAC to COPE", pp. 247, 254.

60. Charles K. McFarland, *Roosevelt, Lewis and the New Deal, 1933–1940* (Fort Worth, Texas: Texas Christian University, 1970), pp. 110, 116. See also Billy H. Wyche, "Southern Attitudes Toward Industrial Unions, 1933–1941," Ph.D. Dissertation, University of Georgia, 1970, especially p. 19.

Notes to THE NEW DEAL AND SOUTHERN POLITICS
by Alan Brinkley

1. V. O. Key, Jr., *Southern Politics in State and Nation* (New York: Alfred A. Knopf, 1949), pp. 3–4.

2. Ibid., p. 645.

3. Henry C. Dethloff, "Missouri Farmers and the New Deal," *Agricultural History* 39 (July 1965), 142–144; J. Wayne Flynt, *Dixie's Forgotten People: The South's Poor Whites* (Bloomington: Indiana University Press, 1979), pp. 78–79.

4. See, e.g., Lyle W. Dorsett, *Franklin D. Roosevelt and the City Bosses* (Port Washington, N.Y.: Kennikat Press, 1977), and Bruce M. Stave, *The New Deal and the Last Hurrah: Pittsburgh Machine Politics* (Pittsburgh: University of Pittsburgh Press, 1970).

5. Paul E. Mertz, *New Deal Policy and Southern Rural Poverty* (Baton Rouge: Louisiana State University Press, 1978), pp. 40–49, 53–54, 61, 83.

6. Theda Skocpol, "Political Response to Capitalist Crisis," *Politics and Society* 10 No. 2 (1980), 155–201; Skocpol and Kenneth Finegold, "State Capacity and Economic Intervention in the New Deal," *Political Science Quarterly* 97 (Summer 1982), 255–278; James T. Patterson, *The New Deal and the States: Federalism in Transition* (Princeton: Princeton University Press, 1969), pp. 201–207.

7. A. Cash Koeniger, "The New Deal and the States: Roosevelt versus the Byrd Organization in Virginia," *Journal of American History* 68 (March 1982), 876–896. According to Koeniger, "The demise of the Price faction was not the fault of its Virginia leaders, whose efforts has been marked by dedication and teamwork throughout. Nor did it result from Virginia's disillusionment with the New Deal. . . . Rather, Roosevelt himself sacrificed the Price faction, denying it the patronage that its leaders frantically insisted they must have to 'save face' in Virginia" after a 1938 electoral setback. Ibid., p. 895. See also Robert F. Hunter, "Virginia and the New Deal," in John Braeman et al., eds., *The New Deal. Volume II: The State and Local Levels* (Columbus: Ohio State University Press, 1975), pp. 103–133; and Hunter, "The AAA Between Neighbors: Virginia, North Carolina, and the New Deal Farm Program," *Journal of Southern History* 44 (November 1978), 537–570.

8. James MacGregor Burns, *Roosevelt: The Lion and the Fox* (New York:

Harcourt, Brace & World, Inc., 1956), pp. 379–380.

9. See, e.g., William G. Carleton, "The Conservative South—A Political Myth," *Virginia Quarterly Review* 22 (Spring 1946), 179–192; Carleton, "The Southern Politician—1900 and 1950," *Journal of Politics* 13 (May 1951), 215–231; Norman Phillips, "The Question of Southern Conservatism," *South Atlantic Quarterly* 54 (January 1955), 1–10; Lee Coller, "The Solid South Cracks," *New Republic* 94 (March 23, 1938), 185–186. Historians who maintain that the New Deal helped sow "seeds of change," but who stop short of the larger claims of Carleton and Phillips, include Frank Freidel, *The New Deal and the South* (Baton Rouge: Louisiana State University Press, 1965), pp. 99–101; George B. Tindall, *The Emergence of the New South, 1913–1945* (Baton Rouge: Louisiana State University Press, 1967), pp. 631–639; and Dewey Grantham, Jr., *The Democratic South* (Athens: University of Georgia Press, 1963), pp. 67–70. Marian D. Irish, "The Southern One-Party System and National Politics," *Journal of Politics* 4 (February 1942), 80–94, offers a contemporary assessment.

10. James W. Dunn, "The New Deal and Florida Politics" (unpublished Ph.D. dissertation, Florida State University, 1971), pp. 169–171, 201; Merlin G. Cox, "David Sholtz: New Deal Governor of Florida," *Florida Historical Quarterly* 43 (October 1964), 142–152.

11. Tindall, *Emergence of the New South*, pp. 726–727.

12. John Temple Graves II, "This is America: III. The South Still Loves Roosevelt." *Nation* 149 (July 1, 1939), 12; *Newsweek*, October 4, 1937, pp. 34–36.

13. U.S. National Emergency Council, *Report on Economic Conditions of the South* (Washington: Government Printing Office, 1938); Tindall, *Emergence of the New South*, pp. 598–600; Tindall, "The 'Colonial Economy' and the Growth Psychology: The South in the 1930s," *South Atlantic Quarterly* 64 (Autumn 1965), 473–474; Mertz, *New Deal and Southern Rural Poverty*, pp. 247–248; Steve Davis, "The South as 'the Nation's No. 1 Economic Problem: The NEC Report of 1938," *Georgia Historical Quarterly* 62 (Summer 1978), 119–131.

14. Patterson, *Congressional Conservatism*, pp. 250–297; James C. Cobb, "Not Gone, But Forgotten: Eugene Talmadge and the 1938 Purge Campaign," *Georgia Historical Quarterly* 59 (Summer 1975), 197–209. Cobb claims that, had Roosevelt not intervened in the race, George might well have been defeated— not by Lawrence Camp, the New Deal candidate whom the President endorsed, but by Eugene Talmadge.

15. "My Party & Myself," *Time*, August 22, 1938, pp. 19–20; "50¢ Fight," ibid., (August 29, 1938); Roy E. Fossett, "The Impact of the New Deal on Georgia Politics, 1933–1941" (unpublished Ph.D. thesis, University of Florida, 1960), pp. 295–306; Tindall, *Emergence of the New South*, p. 629.

16. *Atlanta Constitution*, September 16, 1938. See ibid., September 1, 1938; *Charlotte Observer*, September 1, 1938; "It's a Bust," *Time*, September 26, 1938, p. 13; Patterson, *Congressional Conservatism*, pp. 283–287; J. B. Shannon, "Presidential Politics in the South, 1938, I," *Journal of Politics* 1 (May 1939), 146–170; and Shannon, "Presidential Politics . . . II," ibid., pp. 278–298.

17. *Atlanta Constitution*, September 11, 1938.

18. T. Harry Williams, *Huey Long* (New York: Alfred A. Knopf, 1969), pp. 619–706; Alan Brinkley, *Voices of Protest: Huey Long, Father Coughlin, and the Great Depression* (New York: Alfred A. Knopf, 1982), pp. 36–81, 143–168, 276–283.

19. Ibid., pp. 216–222; A. Wigfall Green, *The Man Bilbo* (Baton Rouge: Louisi-

ana State University Press, 1963), pp. 9–97; William Anderson, *The Wild Man from Sugar Creek* (Baton Rouge: Louisiana State University Press, 1975).

20. Key, *Southern Politics*, p. 645; Tindall, *Emergence of the New South*, p. 649; Patterson, "The Failure of Party Realignment in the South," *Journal of Politics* 27 (August 1965), 617.

21. David Conrad, *The Forgotten Farmer: The Story of the Sharecroppers in the New Deal* (Urbana: University of Illinois Press, 1965), pp. 64–82, 205–209, and passim; Donald H. Grubbs, *Cry From the Cotton: The Southern Tenant Farmers' Union and the New Deal* (Chapel Hill: University of North Carolina Press, 1971), pp. 3–61; Jonathan M. Wiener, "Class Structure and Economic Development in the American South, 1865–1955," *American Historical Review* 84 (October 1979), 970–992.

22. See David Potter, *The South and the Concurrent Majority* (Baton Rouge: Louisiana State University Press, 1972).

23. Ibid., pp. 67–73; John M. Allswang, *The New Deal and American Politics* (New York: John Wiley & Sons, 1978), pp. 53–56, 101–103; Harvard Sitkoff, *A New Deal for Blacks. The Emergence of Civil Rights as a National Issue* (New York: Oxford University Press, 1978), pp. 84–138; Nancy J. Weiss, *Farewell to the Party of Lincoln: Black Politics in the Age of FDR* (Princeton: Princeton University Press, 1983), passim.

24. Other discussions of the relationship between changes in national Democratic politics and the politics of the South in the 1930s include Monroe Lee Billington, *The Political South in the Twentieth Century* (New York: Charles Scribner's Sons, 1975), pp. 67–68; Grantham, *The Democratic South*, pp. 70–75; Potter, *The South and the Concurrent Majority*, pp. 61–89.

25. Patterson, "Failure of Party Realignment in the South," p. 603; Freidel, *FDR and the South*, pp. 91–92.

26. Patterson, *Congressional Conservatism and the New Deal*, p. 20.

Notes to THE IMPACT OF THE NEW DEAL ON BLACK SOUTHERNERS
by Harvard Sitkoff

1. This essay is in part a revision of, and in part a restatement of, some of the themes treated at length in Harvard Sitkoff, *A New Deal For Blacks, The Emergence of Civil Rights as a National Issue, Volume I: The Depression Decade* (New York, 1978). It has been greatly aided by a critique by Professor John B. Kirby, as well as by the ideas he expressed in his *Black Americans in the Roosevelt Era, Liberalism and Race* (Knoxville: University of Tennessee Press, 1980). My work is also much indebted to Professor Raymond Wolters for his extensively researched *Negroes and the Great Depression: The Problem of Economic Recovery* (Westport, Conn.: Greenwood Press, 1970), and incisive "The New Deal and the Negro," in John Braeman, *et al.*, eds., *The New Deal, The National Level* (Columbus, Ohio, 1975), 170–217.

2. Roosevelt is quoted in Walter White, *A Man Called White* (New York, 1948), 169–70. Also see Walter White to Charles Houston, March 9, 1935 and Edwin R. Embree to Walter White, April 16, 1935, NAACP Papers, Library of Congress, Washington, D.C.; Allan Morrison, "The Secret Papers of FDR," *Negro Digest*, 9 (January 1951), 9; Rayford Logan, "The Negro and the National

Recovery Program," *Sphinx*, March 1934, p. 10; Donald H. Grubbs, *Cry From the Cotton, The Southern Tenant Farmers' Union and the New Deal* (Chapel Hill: University of North Carolina Press, 1971), 107, 147–157; Lester C. Lamon, *Blacks in Tennessee, 1791–1970* (Knoxville: University of Tennessee Press, 1981), 91; and Anthony P. Dunbar, *Against the Grain, Southern Radicals and Prophets, 1929–1959* (Charlottesville: University Press of Virginia, 1981), 187.

3. Henry Lee Moon, "Racial Aspects of the Federal Public Relations Programs," *Phylon*, 4 (First Quarter, 1943), 69; Eleanor Roosevelt, *This I Remember* (New York, 1949), 162; and Roy Wilkins, *Oral History Collection*, Butler Library, Columbia University (hereafter cited "COHC"), 98–99. Also see Wolters, *Negroes and the Great Depression*, xi–xiii.

4. Wolters, *ibid.*, 110–112; Robert C. Weaver, "Federal Aid, Local Control, and Negro Participation, *Journal of Negro Education*, 11 (Jan. 1942), 47–59; Lamon, *Blacks in Tennessee*, 88–89; and Ralph J. Bunche, "The Political Status of the Negro" (unpublished manuscript prepared for the Carnegie-Myrdal Study, 1940, Schomburg Branch, New York Public Library), 1414–15. Also see John Dollard, *Caste and Class in a Southern Town* (New Haven: Yale University Press, 1937) and *Children of Bondage: The Personality Development of Negro Youth in the Urban South* (Washington, D.C.: American Council on Education, 1940).

5. John P. Davis, "Blue Eagles and Black Workers," *New Republic*, 91 (Nov. 14, 1934), 7–9; "Negro Complaints Against Codes," *Christian Century*, LI (March 28, 1934), 434; Donald Richberg to Eleanor Roosevelt, Oct. 23, 1934, and Walter White to Franklin Roosevelt, May 21, 1935, NAACP papers; and *Journal and Guide* quote in Leslie H. Fishel, Jr., "The Negro in the New Deal Era," *Wisconsin Magazine of History*, 48 (Winter 1964), 114. Also see Michael S. Holmes, "The Blue Eagle as 'Jim Crow Bird': The NRA and Georgia's Black Workers," *Journal of Negro History*, 67 (July 1972), 276–83; and Allan A. Banks, Jr., "Wage Differentials and the Negro Under the NRA" (M.A. thesis, Howard University, 1938).

6. Thomas J. Woofter, "The Negro and Agricultural Policy" (unpublished memorandum prepared for the Carnegie-Myrdal Study, 1940, Schomburg Branch, New York Public Library), 53–59; E. E. Lewis, "Black Cotton Farmers and the AAA," *Opportunity*, 13 (March 1935), 72–74; Harold Hoffsommer, "The AAA and the Sharecropper," *Social Forces*, 13 (May 1935), 494–502; and Roy Wilkins to Henry Wallace, March 8, 1935 and Walter White to Franklin Roosevelt, Feb. 16, 18, 1935, NAACP Papers. Also see David Eugene Conrad, *The Forgotten Farmers: The Story of Sharecroppers in the New Deal* (Urbana, Ill.: University of Illinois Press, 1965); and Arthur F. Raper, *Preface to Peasantry* (Chapel Hill: University of North Carolina Press, 1936).

7. Cranston Clayton, "The TVA and the Race Problem," *Opportunity*, 12 (April 1934), 111–12; Arthur E. Morgan to Eleanor Roosevelt, Oct. 19, 1934, Eleanor Roosevelt Papers, Franklin D. Roosevelt Library, Hyde Park, New York; J. Max Bond to Walter White, June 4, 1935, and Robert C. Weaver to Arthur E. Morgan, Nov. 12, 1935, NAACP Papers; Charles H. Houston and John P. Davis, "TVA: Lily-White Reconstruction" *Crisis*, 41 (Oct. 1934), 290–91; and John P. Davis, "The Plight of the Negro in the Tennessee Valley," *ibid.*, 42 (Oct. 1935), 294, 315. Also see R. G. Tugwell and E. C. Banfield, "Grass Roots Democracy— Myth or Reality?" *Public Administration Review*, 10 (1950), 47–55.

8. William Pickens, "NRA—'Negro Removal Act'?" *World Tomorrow*, 16

(Sept. 28, 1933), 539–40; Arthur Morgan, *The Making of the TVA* (Buffalo: Pro-
metheus Books, 1974), 74–75; Will Alexander, COHC, 606–08; and Rexford G.
Tugwell, *Roosevelt's Revolution: The First Year—A Personal Perspective* (New
York: MacMillan, 1977), 218. Also see Jesse O. Thomas, "The Negro Looks at the
Alphabet," *Opportunity*, 12 (Jan. 1934), 11–12; and John G. Van Deusen, "The
Negro in Politics," *Journal of Negro History*, 21 (July 1936), 273–74.

9. Walter White to Franklin Roosevelt, July 30, 1935, NAACP Papers; John A.
Salmond, "The Civilian Conservation Corps and the Negro," *Journal of American
History*, 52 (June 1965), 75–88; and Luther C. Wandall, "A Negro in the CCC,"
Crisis, 42 (Sept. 1934), 254.

10. W. J. Trent, Jr., "Federal Sanctions Directed Against Racial Discrimina-
tion," *Phylon*, 3 (Second Quarter, 1942), 171–82; Lorena Hickok to Harry Hop-
kins, Jan. 14, 16, Feb. 8, 14, 18, April 13, 17, 1934 in Lorena Hickok Papers,
Roosevelt Library; Gardner Jackson to Harry Hopkins, Sept. 12, 1936, Franklin
Roosevelt Papers, OF 444-C, Roosevelt Library; Esther Morris Douty, "FERA
and the Rural Negro," *Survey*, 70 (1934), 215–16; and Forrester B. Washington,
"The Negro and Relief," *Proceedings of the National Conference of Social Work*
(Washington, D.C., 1934), 188–90. Also see Richard Sterner, *The Negro's Share*
(New York: Harper, 1943), 218–38.

11. Sterner, *ibid.*, 239–53; Ruth Durant, "Home Rule in the WPA," *Survey*, 75
(Sept. 1939), 274–75; and Donald S. Howard, *The WPA and Federal Relief Policy*
(New York: Russell Sage, 1943), 285–90.

12. Harold Ickes to Walter White, March 1, July 11, 1933, NAACP Papers;
Robert C. Weaver, "An Experiment in Negro Labor," *Opportunity*, 14 (Oct.
1936), 295–98; Marc W. Kruman, "Quotas for Blacks: The Public Works Administration and the Black Construction Worker," *Labor History*, 16 (Winter 1975),
37–49; Robert C. Weaver, "Racial Policy in Public Housing," *Phylon*, 1 (Second
Quarter, 1940), 153–54; and Robert C. Weaver, "The Public Works Administration School Building—Aid Program and Separate Negro Schools," *Journal of
Negro Education*, 7 (July 1938), 366–74.

13. Walter Daniel and Carroll Miller, "The Participation of the Negro in the
National Youth Administration," *ibid.*, 361; Marian Thompson Wright, "Negro
Youth and Federal Emergency Programs: CCC and NYA," *ibid.*, IX (July 1940),
402–05; and Allen F. Kifer, "The Negro Under the New Deal" (Ph.D. diss.,
University of Wisconsin, 1961), 82–83, 127–28.

14. Donald Holley, "The Negro in the New Deal Resettlement Program," *Agricultural History*, 45 (1971), 179–93; Paul E. Mertz, *New Deal Policy and Southern Rural Poverty* (Baton Rouge: Louisiana State University Press, 1978), 193–95;
Sidney Baldwin, *Poverty and Politics: The Rise and Decline of the Farm Security
Administration* (Chapel Hill: University of North Carolina Press, 1968), 193–97,
279; Grubbs, *Cry From the Cotton*, 158; and Dunbar, *Against the Grain*, 184.

15. James T. Patterson, *America's Struggle Against Poverty, 1900–1980* (Cam-
bridge, Mass.: Harvard University Press, 1981), 75–77; John L. Robinson, ed.,
Living Hard: Southern Americans in the Great Depression (Washington, D.C.:
University Press of America, 1981), 103; Mary McLeod Bethune to Franklin
Roosevelt, Oct. 17, 1939, Roosevelt Papers, OF 93, Roosevelt Library; Mary
McLeod Bethune, "I'll Never Turn Back No More!" *Opportunity*, 26 (Nov. 1938),
324–26; W. E. B. DuBois, "Race Relations in the United States, 1917–1947,"
Phylon, 9 (Third Quarter, 1948), 240–41; and Washington, "The Negro and Re-
lief," 190. Also see Andrew Buni, *The Negro in Virginia Politics, 1902–1965*

(Charlottesville: University Press of Virginia), 1967), 113–14; and John Solomon Otto, "Hard Times Blues (1929–1940): Downhome Blues Recordings as Oral Documents," *Oral History Review* (1980), 73–80.

16. Editorials in Baltimore *Afro-American*, April 7, 1934, April 27, 1935, and Norfolk *Journal and Guide*, Oct. 31, 1936; Bunche, "The Political Status of the Negro," 106, 418–19, 427–29; William Brink and Louis Harris, *The Negro Revolution in America* (New York: Simon & Schuster, 1964), 90; Rayford W. Logan, ed., *The Attitude of the Southern White Press Toward Negro Suffrage, 1932–1940* (Washington, D.C.: The Foundation Publishers, 1940), 62–66; Howard W. Odum, *Race and Rumors of Race: Challenge to American Crisis* (Chapel Hill: University of North Carolina Press, 1943), 81; and Walter White to William Pickens, Nov. 9, 1932, and Walter White to Claude A. Barnett, Nov. 11, 1932, NAACP Papers.

17. Laurence J. W. Hayes, *The Negro Federal Government Worker: A Study of His Classification Status in the District of Columbia: 1883–1938* (Washington, D.C.: The Graduate School, Howard University, 1941), 73, 153; Gunnar Myrdal, *An American Dilemma: The Negro Problem and Modern Democracy* (New York: Harper, 1944), 503; Roy Wilkins, COHC, 68–69; Jane R. Motz, "The Black Cabinet: Negroes in the Administration of Franklin D. Roosevelt" (Master's Thesis, U. of Delaware, 1964), 34–36; and Bunche, "Political Status of the Negro," 1359–78, quote at 1361.

18. William Birnie, "Black Brain Trust," *American Magazine*, 135 (Jan. 1943), 36–37, 94–95; Will Alexander, COHC, 369; Motz, "The Black Cabinet," *op. cit.*; Wilkins, COHC, 68; *Opportunity*, 15 (March 1937), 69; and B. Joyce Ross, "Mary McLeod Bethune and the National Youth Administration: A Case Study of Power Relationships in the Black Cabinet of Franklin D. Roosevelt," *Journal of Negro History*, 60 (Jan. 1975), 28.

19. "Black on Blacks," *Time*, 27 (April 27, 1936), 10–11, and "Black Game," *ibid.*, XXVIII (Aug. 17, 1936), 10–11; Heywood Broun, "Roosevelt Comes Up Swinging," *Nation*, 143 (July 4, 1936), 9; *New York Times*, Oct. 27, 1936; "The Democratic Convention," *Opportunity*, 14 (July 1936), 197; Pittsburgh *Courier*, July 13, 20, 27, 1940; Chicago *Defender*, Oct. 19, 26, Nov. 2, 1940; editorial, Norfolk *Journal and Guide*, Nov. 2, 1940; Myrdal, *An American Dilemma*, 488; Lee Collier, "The Solid South Cracks," *New Republic*, 92 (March 23, 1938), 185–86; Larry W. Dunn, "Knoxville Negro Voting and the Roosevelt Revolution, 1928–1936," *East Tennessee Historical Society's Publications*, 43 (1971), 87; Angus Campbell, et al., *The American Voter* (New York: Wiley, 1960), 153–54; Kristi Anderson, *The Creation of a Democratic Majority, 1928–1936* (Chicago: University of Chicago Press, 1979), xii; and Bunche, "Political Status of the Negro," 307–317, 325–26, 422–24, 444–46.

20. Frank Freidel, *F.D.R. and the South* (Baton Rouge: Louisiana State University Press, .1965), 97; editorial, Pittsburgh *Courier*, April 20, 1935; editorial, Chicago *Defender*, Oct. 13, 1934; column by David W. Howe, *ibid.*, Feb. 3, 1940; and Walter White to Rexford Tugwell, July 26, 1935, and William Hastie to Walter White, Jan. 4, 1939, NAACP Papers.

21. Will Alexander, COHC, 258; Bernard Nelson, "The Negro Before the Supreme Court," *Phylon*, 8 (First Quarter 1947), 34–38; Milton R. Knovitz, "A Nation Within a Nation—the Negro and the Supreme Court," *American Scholar*, 11 (Jan. 1941), 69–78; and Raymond Pace Alexander, "The Upgrading of the Negro's Status by Supreme Court Decisions," *Journal of Negro History*, 30 (April 1945), 137.

22. Roy Wilkins with Tom Mathews, *Standing Fast: The Autobiography of Roy Wilkins* (New York: Viking Press, 1982), 130–31; *Opportunity*, 12 (June 1934), 167, and XIV (Jan. 1936), 5; Joseph Lash, *Eleanor Roosevelt: A Friend's Memoir* (Garden City, N.Y.: Doubleday, 1964), 168–69; *Crisis*, 46 (Feb. 1939), 54, and (Sept. 1939), 265; Odum, *Race and Rumors of Race*, 81; and editorials in Baltimore *Afro-American*, April 7, 1934, April 27, 1935, May 23, 1936, Philadelphia *Independent*, Feb. 20, 1938, Pittsburgh *Courier*, Dec. 3, 1938, and Chicago *Defender*, March 4, 1939.

23. Eleanor Roosevelt, "Some of My Best Friends Are Negro," *Ebony*, 8 (Feb. 1953), 26; Joseph P. Lash, *Eleanor and Franklin* (New York: Signet Books, 1971), 671–77; Eli Ginzberg and Alfred S. Eichner, *The Troublesome Presence, American Democracy and the Negro* (Glencoe, Ill.: The Free Press of Glencoe, 1964), 293; Freidel, *F.D.R. and the South*, 98; *New York Times*, Sept. 10, 1938; W. E. B. Du Bois, "Roosevelt," *Crisis*, 41 (Jan. 1934), 20; Baltimore *Afro-American*, April 16, 1938; L. C. Dyer to Walter White, Jan. 28, 1935, "Memorandum on Interview of the Secretary of the N.A.A.C.P. with the President at the White House on January 2, 1936," and Walter White to William Hastie, April 15, 1938, NAACP Papers; Wolters, *Negroes and the Great Depression*, 302–52, 365–66; Roy Wilkins, COHC, 70–71, 75–76; Walter White to Eleanor Roosevelt, Dec. 23, 1938, Eleanor Roosevelt Papers; and Henry A. Schweinhaut, "The Civil Liberties Section of the Department of Justice," *Bill of Rights Review*, 1 (1940–41), 206–07.

24. Editorial in Philadelphia *Tribune*, Oct. 27, 1938; Mary McLeod Bethune, "I'll Never Turn Back No More!" *Opportunity*, 16 (Nov. 1938), 324–26; William Hastie to Franklin Roosevelt, Feb. 11, 1939, NAACP Papers; Dewey W. Grantham, *The Democratic South* (Athens: University of Georgia Press, 1963), 74, 96; Morton Sosna, *In Search of the Silent South, Southern Liberals and the Race Issue* (New York: Columbia University Press, 1977), chs. 4–5; and August Meier and Elliot Rudwick, "The Origins of Nonviolent Direct Action in Afro-American Protest: A Note on Historical Discontinuities," in their *Along the Color Line, Explorations in the Black Experience* (Urbana, Ill.: University of Illinois Press, 1976), esp. 314–344. Also see Clark Foreman, "The Decade of Hope." *Phylon*, 12 (Second Quarter, 1951), 137–50; H. C. Nixon, "The New Deal and the South," *Virginia Quarterly Review*, 19 (Summer 1943), 321–33; and Charles S. Johnson, "More Southerners Discover the South," *Crisis*, 41 (Jan. 1939), 14–15.

25. "Franklin D. Roosevelt," *ibid.*, LII (May 1945), 129; Adam Clayton Powell, Jr., *Marching Blacks* (New York, 1945), 116–18; editorial in Norfolk *Journal and Guide*, April 21, 1945; Myrdal, *An American Dilemma*, 74, 1022; Rackham Holt, *Mary McLeod Bethune* (Garden City: Doubleday, 1964), 182; Walter White to Daisy Lampkin, June 23, 1938, NAACP Papers; and Lerone Bennett, Jr., *Confrontation: Black and White* (New York: Johnson Publishing Co., 1965), 142. Also see "Conclusion" in Richard Wright, *12 Million Black Voices* (New York, 1941); E. Franklin Frazier, "Sociological Theory and Race Relations," *American Sociological Review*, 12 (June 1947), 265–71; Charles S. Johnson, *et al.*, *Into the Mainstream, A Survey of Best Practices in Race Relations in the South* (Chapel Hill: University of North Carolina Press, 1947) *passim;* and Lyonel Florant, "Youth Exhibits a New Spirit," *Crisis*, 43 (Aug. 1936), 237–38, 253–54.

Notes to THE NEW DEAL AS A TURNING POINT IN SOUTHERN
HISTORY
by Numan V. Bartley

1. I. A. Newby, The South, A History (New York: Holt, Rinehart and Winston,
1978), p. 302; John Samuel Ezell, The South Since 1865 (New York: Macmillan,
1963), p. 102. The classic statement of this interpretation was, of course, C. Vann
Woodward, Origins of the New South, 1877–1913 (Baton Rouge: Louisiana State
University Press, 1951).
    2. William Faulkner, Intruder in the Dust (New York: Random House, 1948),
p. 99.
    3. Some of the best of this literature is reprinted in Patrick Gerster and
Nicholas Cords, eds., Myth and Southern History (Chicago: Rand McNally Col-
lege Publishing, 1974).
    4. George Brown Tindall, The Ethnic Southerners (Baton Rouge: Louisiana
State University Press, 1976), p. 224; V. O. Key, Jr., Southern Politics in State
and Nation (New York: Alfred A. Knopf, 1949), p. 664. See James C. Cobb,
"Urbanization and the Changing South: A Review of the Literature," South Atlantic Urban Studies 1 (1977): 253–66.
    5. Eric Foner, Nothing But Freedom: Emancipation and Its Legacy (Baton
Rouge: Louisiana State University Press, 1983), p. 6.
    6. The historiography on the New South is discussed more fully in Numan V.
Bartley, "Another New South?," Georgia Historical Quarterly 65 (Summer 1981):
119–37, and Bartley, "In Search of the New South: Southern Politics After Recon-
struction," Reviews in American History 10 (December 1982): 150–63.
    7. Pete Daniel, "The Metamorphosis of Slavery, 1865–1900," Journal of
American History 66 (June 1979): 88–99; Gilbert C. Fite, "Southern Agriculture
Since the Civil War: An Overview," Agricultural History 53 (January 1979): 4;
Jack Temple Kirby, "The Transformation of Southern Plantations, c. 1920–1960,"
Agricultural History 57 (July 1983): 257.
    8. Andrew Nelson Lytle, "The Hind Tit," in I'll Take My Stand: The South and
the Agrarian Tradition, ed. Twelve Southerners (1930; reprint ed., Baton Rouge:
Louisiana State University Press, 1977), p. 217.
    9. W. Arthur Lewis, "Economic Development with Unlimited Supplies of
Labour," in The Economics of Underdevelopment, ed. A. N. Agarwala and S. P.
Singh (London: Oxford University Press, 1958), p. 408; Samuel P. Huntington,
Political Order in Changing Societies (New Haven: Yale University Press, 1968),
p. 72.
    10. "Master Cain of the Grover Cleveland," interviewed by Lawrence F.
Evans, 1 November 1938, Federal Writers Project, Box 9, Southern Historical
Collection, University of North Carolina, Chapel Hill.
    11. Edward Atkinson, "The South and Its Development," Tradesman Annual,
1895, pp. 176–77.
    12. Blaine A. Brownell, The Urban Ethos in the South, 1920–1930 (Baton
Rouge: Louisiana State University Press, 1975), p. xvi, passim.
    13. W. J. Cash, The Mind of the South (New York: Alfred A. Knopf, 1941),
p. 205.
    14. Eric Foner, Free Soil, Free Labor, Free Men: The Ideology of the Repub-
lican Party Before the Civil War (New York: Oxford University Press, 1970),
pp. 1–62; Daniel T. Rogers, The Work Ethic in Industrial America, 1850–1920

(Chicago: University of Chicago Press, 1978), pp. 1–64.

15. Karl Polanyi, *The Great Transformation: The Political and Economic Origins of Our Time* (1944; reprint ed., Boston: Beacon Press, 1970), p. 163.

16. James C. Cobb, *The Selling of the South: The Southern Crusade for Industrial Development, 1936–1980* (Baton Rouge: Louisiana State University Press, 1982).

17. Leslie W. Dunbar, "The Changing Mind of the South: The Exposed Nerve," *Journal of Politics* 26 (February 1964): 20.

18. National Emergency Council, *Report on Economic Conditions of the South* (Washington: Government Printing Office, 1938), p. 1.

19. Richard Klimmer, "Liberal Attitudes Toward the South, 1930–1965" (Ph.D. dissertation, Northwestern University, 1976), pp. 125–52.

20. Cleanth Brooks, *William Faulkner: First Encounters* (New Haven: Yale University Press, 1983), p. 77.

21. Richard H. King, *A Southern Renaissance: The Cultural Awakening of the American South, 1930–1955* (New York: Oxford University Press, 1980), p. 291. And see Daniel Joseph Singal, *The War Within: From Victorian to Modernist Thought in the South, 1919–1945* (Chapel Hill: University of North Carolina Press, 1982), p. 8.

22. Leonard Michaels, *The Men's Club* (New York: Farrar, Straus and Giroux, 1978), p. 4.

23. Reinhard Bendix, "Tradition and Modernity Reconsidered," *Comparative Studies in Society and History* 9 (April, 1967): 319.

24. Marshall Frady, *Southerners: A Journalist's Odyssey* (New York: New American Library, 1980), p. 281.

25. Quoted in *Atlanta Constitution*, 1 February 1982, p. B2.

26. Neil Shister, "Who Owns Atlanta?," *Atlanta* 20 (January 1981): 51.

27. David R. Goldfield, "The Urban South: A Regional Framework," *American Historical Review*, 86 (December, 1981): 1009–1034.

28. Cobb, *The Selling of the South*, p. 267.

29. Flannery O'Connor, "The Fiction Writer and His Country," in *The Living Novel: A Symposium*, ed. Granville Hicks (New York: Macmillan, 1957), p. 159.

30. John Shelton Reed, *Southerners: The Social Psychology of Sectionalism* (Chapel Hill: University of North Carolina Press, 1983), pp. 31–50.

31. Bendix, "Tradition and Modernity Reconsidered," p. 319.

Selected Bibliography

The purpose of this selected bibliography is to provide the reader with a general guide to the literature on the New Deal and the South. It is not designed nor intended to be a complete listing. Readers are directed to check the notes to each essay for exact sources used by each individual author.

General Works

Bartley, Numan. "Another New South?" *Georgia Historical Quarterly* 65 (Summer 1981), 119–37.

Braeman, John, et al., eds., *The New Deal: The State and Local Levels*. Columbus, Ohio: Ohio State University Press, 1975.

Ezell, John S. *The South since 1865*. New York: Macmillan, 1963.

Freidel, Frank. *FDR and the South*. Baton Rouge: Louisiana State University Press, 1965.

National Emergency Council. *Report on the Economic Conditions of the South*. Washington, D.C.: Government Printing Office, 1938.

Newby, I.A. *The South: A History*. New York: Holt, Rinehart, and Winston, 1978.

Patterson, James T. *The New Deal and the States: Federalism in Transition*. Princeton: Princeton University Press, 1969.

Tindall, George. *The Emergence of the New South, 1913–1945*. Baton Rouge, Louisiana State University Press, 1967.

Economic Policy

Baldwin, Sidney. *Poverty and Politics: The Rise and Decline of the Farm Security Administration*. Chapel Hill: University of North Carolina Press, 1967.

Conkin, Paul. *Tomorrow a New World: The New Deal Community Program*. Ithaca, New York: Cornell University Press, 1959.

Conrad, David. *The Forgotten Farmers: The Story of Sharecroppers in the New Deal*. Urbana, Illinois: University of Illinois Press, 1965.

Daniel, Pete. "Transformation of the Rural South, 1930 to the Present." *Agricultural History* 55 (July 1981), 231–248.

Grubbs, Donald H. *Cry from the Cotton: The Southern Tenant Farmers' Union and the New Deal*. Chapel Hill: University of North Carolina Press, 1971.

Holley, Donald. *Uncle Sam's Farmers: The New Deal Communities in the Lower Mississippi Valley*. Urbana, Illinois: University of Illinois Press, 1975.

Kirby, Jack Temple. "The Transformation of Southern Plantations, c. 1920–1960." *Agricultural History* 57 (July 1983), 257–276.

Mertz, Paul. *New Deal Policy and Southern Rural Poverty*. Baton Rouge: Louisiana State University Press, 1978.

Musoke, Moses. "Mechanizing Cotton Production in the American South: The Tractor, 1915–1960." *Explorations in Economic History* 18 (October 1981), 347–375.

Perkins, Van L. *Crisis in Agriculture: The Agricultural Adjustment Administration and the New Deal*. Berkeley, California: University of California Press, 1969.

Labor

Auerbach, Jerold. *Labor and Liberty: The LaFollette Committee and the New Deal*. Indianapolis: Bobbs-Merrill, 1966.

Bernstein, Irving. *Turbulent Years: A History of the American Worker, 1933–1941*. Boston, Massachusetts: Houghton-Mifflin, 1969.

Brody, David. "Labor and the Great Depression: The Interpretive Prospects." *Labor History* 13 (Spring 1972), 231–244.

Derber, Milton and Edwin Young, eds. *Labor and the New Deal*. Madison, Wisconsin: University of Wisconsin Press, 1957.

Fink, Gary and Merl Reed, eds. *Essays in Southern Labor History*. Westport, Connecticut: Greenwood Press, 1976.

Flynt, Wayne. "A Vignette in Southern Labor Politics—The 1936 Mississippi Senatorial Primary." *Mississippi Quarterly: The Journal of Southern Culture* 26 (Winter 1972–73), 89–99.

Galenson, Walter. *The CIO Challenge to the AFL: A History of the American Labor Movement, 1935–1941*. Cambridge, Massachusetts: Harvard University Press, 1960.

Hevener, John W. *Which Side Are You On? The Harlan County Coal Miners, 1931–1939*. Urbana, Illinois: University of Illinois Press, 1978.

Holmes, Michael. "The Blue Eagle as 'Jim Crow Bird': The NRA and Georgia Black Workers." *Journal of Negro History* 57 (July 1972), 276–283.

Olson, James. "Organized Black Leadership and Industrial Unionism: The Racial Response, 1936–1945." *Labor History* 10 (Summer 1969), 475–486.

Politics

Anderson, William. *The Wild Man from Sugar Creek*. Baton Rouge: Louisiana State University Press, 1975.

Brinkley, Alan. *Voices of Protest: Huey Long, Father Coughlin, and the Great Depression*. New York: Alfred Knopf, 1982.

Cobb, James. "Not Gone, but Forgotten: Eugene Talmadge and the 1938 Purge Campaign." *Georgia Historical Quarterly* 59 (Summer 1975), 197–209.

Dorsett, Lyle. *Franklin D. Roosevelt and the City Bosses*. Port Washington, New York: Kennikat Press, 1977.

Grantham, Dewey. *The Democratic South*. Athens, Georgia: University of Georgia Press, 1963.

Key. V. O. *Southern Politics in State and Nation*. New York: Alfred Knopf, 1949.

Koeniger, A. Cash. "The New Deal and the States: Roosevelt Versus the Byrd Organization in Virginia." *Journal of American History* 68 (March 1982), 876–896.

Patterson, James T. *Congressional Conservatism and the New Deal*. Lexington, Kentucky: University of Kentucky Press, 1967.

Williams, T. Harry. *Huey Long*. New York: Alfred Knopf, 1969.

Black Southerners

Fishel, Leslie S. "The Negro and the New Deal," in Alonzo Hamby, ed. *The New Deal: Analysis and Interpretation*. Second Edition. New York: Longman, 1981.

Harris, William H. *Keeping the Faith: A. Philip Randolph, Milton P. Webster, and the Brotherhood of Sleeping Car Porters, 1925–1937*. Urbana, Illinois: University of Illinois Press, 1977.

Holt, Rackham. *Mary McLeod Bethune*. Garden City: Doubleday, 1964.

Kirby, John B. *Black Americans in the Roosevelt Era: Liberalism and Race*. Knoxville, Tennessee: University of Tennessee Press, 1980.

Lash, Joseph. *Eleanor and Franklin*. New York: Signet Book, 1971.

Myrdal, Gunnar. *An American Dilemma, the Negro Problem and Modern Democracy*. New York: Harper, 1944.

Sitkoff, Harvard. *A New Deal for Blacks, The Emergence of Civil Rights as a National Issue. Volume I: The Depression Decade*. New York: Oxford University Press, 1978.

Terrill, Tom and Jerrold Hirsch, eds. *Such As Us: Southern Voices of the Thirties*. New York: W. W. Norton, 1979.

Wolters, Raymond. *Negroes and the Great Depression: The Problem of Economic Recovery*. Westport, Connecticut: Greenwood Press, 1970.

Contributors

Frank Freidel is Bullitt Professor of American history at the University of Washington. His works include a 4-volume biography of *Franklin D. Roosevelt* and *F.D.R. and the South*.

Pete Daniel is Curator of the Division of Extractive Industries at the National Museum of American History in Washington, D.C. He has written *Deep'n as it Come: The 1927 Mississippi River Flood* and *The Shadow of Slavery: Peonage in the South, 1901–1969*.

J. Wayne Flynt is the Head of the Department of History and Hollifield Professor of Southern History at Auburn University. He has written several articles on southern labor and his best known study is *Dixie's Forgotten People: The South's Poor Whites*.

Alan Brinkley is Dunwalke Associate Professor of American History at Harvard University. He is the author of *Voices of Protest: Huey Long, Father Coughlin, and the Great Depression*.

Harvard Sitkoff is Professor of History at the University of New Hampshire. His publications include *A New Deal for Blacks, the Emergence of Civil Rights as a National Issue: Volume I, The Depression Decade*, and *The Struggle for Black Equality, 1954–1980*.

Numan V. Bartley is Professor of History at the University of Georgia. He is the author of several books, including *The Rise of Massive Resistance: Race and Politics in the South during the 1950s* and *From Thurmond to Wallace: Political Tendencies in Georgia, 1948–1968*.

Index

CPSIA information can be obtained at www.ICGtesting.com
Printed in the USA
LVOW081134280911

248241LV00001B/29/P